PROCESSING TRAUMA

ESE STACEY

PROCESSING TRAUMA
THROUGH BREATH AND MEDITATION

L'EAU VIVE

ISBN 978-1-912156-98-6

Typeset by Stefan Leszczuk at www.szcz.uk

ACKNOWLEDGEMENTS

I'd like to say a thank you to the people that have made this short but important book possible. Self-publishing is never a one-person show. I am immensely grateful to my beautiful friend Michaela who proofread the book, made suggestions for changes and edited the first offerings. I'd like to thank Matt De Bono who has been with me since the beginning of my writing career, starting with the bestselling medical series *Hot Topics in General Practice*. For this current book Matt set up my self-publishing team and guided me along the way, even when on holiday. Stefan has brought the whole project together by proofreading and editing again, typesetting and arranging the final work. Last but not least are my patients and individuals whose emotions and pain shaped this book. Your experiences will be healing for those who read it.

To all those who are walking this journey to the deeper, Higher Self

Contents

Videos

My YouTube channel is www.youtube.com/@doctorese7079.
Or you can just go to YouTube and search for **doctorese**.

Here are quick links for the YouTube videos I mention in the book:

page 10
The Best You
tinyurl.com/doctorese1

pages 11 and page 24
We forgot to breathe (with Barbara Pidgeon)
tinyurl.com/doctorese2

page 20
Meditations: Helping you to breath and be in touch with your body
tinyurl.com/doctorese3

Introduction

What is trauma? In its simplest form trauma is an injury; in fact the Greek word *trauma* means 'wound'. The injury may be either physical or emotional. A physical trauma may result in or be linked to an emotional trauma. In this book I'm dealing with the emotional trauma. We all experience emotional trauma of varying degrees. The way we respond to an emotional injury differs from person to person. Two people who experience the same insult will respond in different ways. For one person the insult may be negligible, for the other person the insult may have deep and long-lasting effects. In this book I will teach you how to recognise trauma in your own body. After you've learned to recognise this trauma that is locked away somehow in your very being, I then help you to process it. I help you to process the trauma using meditation.

In its simplest terms meditation is an activity of focused attention and relaxation which may lead to altered states of consciousness. Contrast this with today's media-packed world. The ever-present mobile phone is the centre of our flitting attention. It offers many differing experiences at the swipe of the thumb or the tap of the finger. Our brain activity is never still. However, the mobile phone, or video game activity, is a type of meditation. The feedback is addictive and we can get withdrawal symptoms when we don't have it by our sides. Some mobile phone software is written specifically to entice our attention – some with good intentions and others not.[1] The aim of this book is the antithesis of the mobile phone activity. By focusing our attention on the body and not the external world we can lead ourselves to the healing of our locked-in trauma. This is important as suppressed trauma provokes unpredictable behaviour, errant decision making, physical dis-order and eventually dis-ease.*

The book is a distillation of what I currently do with my patients to help them to live their *Best Life*. It is primarily a practical guide that leads you through the steps in meditation that allow you to reach a point where you can 'process' or 'let go' of trauma. However, I have also included some theory and explanations for why I do what I do. Before you delve into the book, let me explain how I arrived at the point of writing it as well as what you can expect to find in the following chapters.

How I started

I trained to become a medical doctor at St Mary's Hospital Medical School in London, United Kingdom. It was like a dream for me when I first walked through the gates of the medical school in Paddington. I was nineteen years old, fresh-faced and eager to pursue my chosen career. I had always loved sport and was ranked within the top 10 for my sport, heptathlon. I wanted to pursue a career in Sports Medicine and help elite sports people. I pursued this dream by first qualifying as a general practitioner and then going on to do a Master of Sports Medicine degree at the Royal London Hospital. I loved the year-long course working with sports people and understanding how to attain and maintain peak fitness. I completed research looking at bone loss in athletic women who had stopped menstruating. I noticed that in many of these women nutrition played a significant part in the cessation of their menstrual periods. During my master's degree we were taught modules in

---

* I have written *dis-ease* and *dis-order* like this deliberately – as the opposites of ease and order.

nutrition and acupuncture, areas that general medical graduates were not taught. This greatly stimulated my interest into finding out more about these so-called complementary forms of medical practice. One of my general practice patients asked if I could prescribe a homeopathic remedy for her son instead of conventional therapy. I was challenged by this as I knew nothing about homeopathy. I told her as much and later she came back with articles and information about a course for doctors at the Royal London Homeopathic hospital (now the Royal London Hospital for Integrated Medicine). Not only did I attend the fascinating introductory course, I ended up taking a postgraduate primary care certificate in homeopathy at the same institution.

After several more years working in general practice and elite sport I went back to the Royal London Hospital as Senior Clinical Lecturer supervising students of master's degrees as I had done years earlier. I also wrote books for general practitioners to help them keep up with current research. These books – called *Hot Topics in General Practice* – were regularly in the *British Medical Journal* bestsellers' book list. In order to write these books I was required to read hundreds of research journals for each topic covered. Each year I would update the series with a new book containing summaries of up-to-date research. I was increasingly fascinated by the research that looked at the effects of nutrition and herbal medicines on health.

When my children came along, I was still fascinated about research and nutrition. As I have described in my previous book, *Diet to Detox* (see page 93) my three children all presented with significant health challenges but standard medical training didn't help me to support them through these difficulties. As time went by it became clear that gut health played a major role in their wellbeing. I began to change their diets and pay particular attention to gut health by introducing fermented foods; this approach greatly helped my children. I then began trying this approach with my patients. By this time I was working in the private health sector close to Harley Street, the private medical district of London. My patients at this point tended to have chronic muscle, tendon and joint problems. I was part of a team of doctors who were sent patients who were particularly difficult to treat as they had already been seen by several orthopaedic specialists. Many of these patients had already tried physiotherapy, injections and sometimes surgery. I began to notice symptoms of gut problems in some of them. In *Diet to Detox*, I explain how poor gut health creates inflammation in the body which can manifest, among other things, as chronic bone, joint and muscle pain. I asked some of the patients to try a change in diet to see if this would help their joints. Some thought I was crazy, others were so desperate for anything to help they were willing to give it go. I would say around half of those original patients found some relief with the gut-based approach to managing chronic bone, joint and muscle problems. As I did further self-study on the topic, I was able to refine my ideas about the gut and health in general. *Diet to Detox* is a culmination of around 20 years of lived experience and theoretic research. It is now clear from research that the gut is intimately related to inflammation, which in turn is intimately related to pain. I became pretty good at spotting gut symptoms and therefore I felt I was able to target the offer of *Diet to Detox* to the appropriate people. However, what I hadn't appreciated was that *Diet to Detox* wouldn't help everyone I expected it to help. There were people who just seemed to get stuck and others who didn't even get past first base. Why? I came to understand that if someone didn't respond in the first few weeks of trying *Diet to Detox*, then they were unlikely to. What was preventing people from progressing?

I used to think that the diet was very straightforward. You eliminate toxic foods for six weeks, you shore up the gut and then reintroduce the foods – Bingo! But some people simply could not manage it, so I began to listen more carefully and pay closer attention to these patients.

One thing that struck me was their reaction to not being able to follow the diet. There were often tears, usually after the first week or so. The most prevalent reaction, however, was anger. This road block in the journey to health that manifested itself as tears, anger and frustration baffled me at first until I began to see that what was manifesting was part of something deeper than a reaction to giving up a favourite food. Once I began to pick up on this reaction, I used to send the patients to see my dear friend Sigi Lower (www.sigilower.com). Sigi is a beautiful soul who talks to horses; she is a horse whisperer. She helps owners who are having difficulty with behavioural issues with their horses. Simply by touching, she can pick up the source of the issue. I remember one story she told me. The owner said that the horse had become aggressive. Sigi saw the horse and worked her usual 'magic' and told the owner that the best course of action was for the owner to sell the horse. The owner was a little perturbed and asked why. Sigi told the owner that some time in the past, he had kicked the horse and this had set up a resentment that would be difficult to unravel. In a similar way to horses, Sigi also works with humans. By touch and just by hearing someone speak, she will get flashes of very accurate intuition leading directly to the root cause of the illness.

It is my belief that all illness has an emotional or psychological root cause. The emotional dis-ease creates an ideal environment in the body that 'attracts' toxins. Toxins then injure the gut and inflammation is created. So it seemed to me that the emotional response I was seeing in some of my patients was in fact a distress signal. Food, as we know, is a great pacifier. Foods can cover up emotional grief very well. We can all find our favourite snack that plugs the hole at the least sign of distress. With *Diet to Detox*, your diet is stripped right back and there is very little space for comfort food. But the joint and other issues do get better. However, it would seem that for those with locked-in trauma, the need to cover the emotional distress is greater than the need to get rid of the pain. What the psyche is trying to say is, 'Help me! My pain goes deeper than the joint.' I would suggest these patients go and see Sigi. My patients love Sigi. She often offers a massage. During the massage, at certain points in their body, she will tune in to relevant information which she then relays to the patient which often results in an unlocking of that deep wound, thus allowing it to heal. After this I would then be able to continue with *Diet to Detox* unhindered by the road block.

I'm a lifelong learner and became intrigued by these emotional road blocks. One day, I was helping a patient who had chronic ill health because of toxins discharging from tooth cavitations. I was trying to find information about jaw cavitations for the patient so that she could give it to her dentist. Most standard dentists think that you mean *cavities* when you talk about *cavitations*. A cavitation is not a hole in the tooth that needs to be filled but a hole in the jaw bone that appears usually as a result of root canal treatments. The hole can become infected, but at a very low level so that it is not really noticed. However, the hole can be a cause of chronic ill health. Cavitations are very difficult to treat and most standard dentists don't even believe that they exist. Anyway, while looking for this information, I stumbled across a research paper that said a particular type of non-physical therapy was able to improve these cavitations. I was curious about this and researched the therapy. Neuromodulation Therapy, or NMT, uses kinesiology to 'ask' the patient's body where the root cause of the illness is (see www.nmt.md). NMT claims to speak directly to the patient's subconscious. Kinesiology, for those who have never heard of it, is a type of muscle testing. As far as I can work out, the muscle testing works a little like a biological lie detector test. You ask the body a question and test the strength of the muscle. Normally, if you ask someone to hold out their arm and keep it strong, and then try to press down on it with two fingers, the muscle will stay strong. The strong deltoid muscle is not troubled by two fingers and will easily remain strong. If you then ask a question to the patient, the answer to which is 'No', and then press down on the strong healthy arm, that same arm will be as weak as a feather. For example, if the person's name is Vera and I ask her to repeat, 'My name is Vera', the arm will remain strong. If I ask Vera to repeat, 'My name is Suzie', the arm will go weak. I don't really know the exact mechanisms behind this phenomenon but I believe it has something to do with the autonomic nervous system and particularly the vagus nerve. Kinesiology was not new to me, but what was new was that you didn't need to ask the question out loud so that the patient could hear it. In NMT you address the question to the patient's subconscious, so you can ask the question in your head. Of course, I found this fascinating and went on to do the full training course.

I love NMT. The information that comes up is always very helpful and sometimes key to progression in a patient with chronic ill health. Patients will often forget emotional trauma. This is the body's mechanism to allow the person to continue with normal life. On a number of occasions the NMT chart has highlighted post-traumatic stress disorder (PTSD). This may not immediately appear on the chart but usually after we have been working together for a few weeks. Again I believe the subconscious knows when the time is right to reveal the deeper hurts. Quite often when I ask the patient about the PTSD, it is then that they recover the memory of the abuse or trauma. NMT then helps the patient to have a smoother journey out of this situation. NMT sessions need to happen on a regular basis until the issue is resolved. Too long in between sessions and the improvement tends to wane. In between NMT sessions I find that if I give patients some *inner (psychological) work* to do, they improve or maintain their level. I often find that some of the road blocks for most patients are the negative internal conversations, what I call the 'stuck record'. The patient might be able to have a positive outlook for brief periods, perhaps during a consultation, but almost immediately the consultation is done, the 'voices' would be back: 'Oh, I wouldn't believe what she says, you've been sick all this time, why would that change?' Or something like, 'Everyone in your family has a bad back, what makes you so different?'

Another obstacle to progress is that patients find it very difficult to *visualise* a positive future. If I ask them the question 'What does the "best you" look like?' they generally are not able to tell me without including the word 'no' or 'pain' in their response. For example they might say, 'The best me has *no pain*. I want to get rid of this *pain* more than anything.' You might say that there's nothing wrong with that answer but if I'm trying to imagine what that patient with no pain looks like, it is very difficult unless they tell me in some detail what it looks/feels/sounds like. Does 'no pain' mean that they are dancing, rock climbing or in their best suit going to work with a smile on their face every day? If you can't 'frame up'/imagine an image of what no pain looks like then neither can the subconscious. If the subconscious can't do it then it won't happen. So, I need to spend some time to help patients 'frame'/see an image of what the *Best Me* looks like for them. I have a YouTube presentation of how to do this (details on page 1).

This does work quite well if the traumas are not too many or too deep. However, I kept feeling that something more was needed as patients with deeper traumas or emotional hurts find it difficult to stick with the *Best You* affirmations. I then began to look at breathing and meditation. I have done some form of meditation all my adult life. I was first taught to meditate when I was 19 years old. It was my first term at medical school and I joined the Catholic society. The priest in charge of the students was a monk who taught us all how to meditate and I have continued on and off ever since. Although I loved the silence of contemplative meditation, over the years I went through different phases of Christian prayer practice. After the initial meditation phase, I went through what I'll call an African Christian phase. I was part of wonderful, large African church. Prayers here are loud and powerful. In the church that I was a member of, you weren't allowed to pray any old prayers off the top of your head, you had to pray using a scripture as the base. I was a deacon in this very large church and when asked to pray you were handed a microphone. No one wanted to be embarrassed by not knowing scripture. As well as that, you were often given the topic you were going to pray about. This meant you had to be prepared with scripture on any manner of subjects so as to be ready for when the microphone came your way. You can bet that I learned scripture very well! After this phase of my Christian journey, I moved back again to a more mystical perspective and the scripture I'd learned became very useful. The Christian mystics tend to take a broader and deeper view of scripture and especially use Hebrew interpretations to give a different perspective on traditional Christian texts.

It was around this time I met my friend Barbara who taught me more about the science of breathing. You can find our interview on my YouTube playlist (details on page 1). After speaking with Barbara, I was astounded that as a sport and exercise medicine consultant I was unfamiliar with the concepts she presented to me. I went on to research further into *Buteyko* and the *Wim Hoff* style of breathing. I attended a Wim Hoff seminar and plunged myself into icy water. I caught the ice water swimming bug and when the weather was too warm, I would put ice in the bath and sit and meditate in the water for up to 40 minutes. I find it really hard to believe that I did this. I now live in Ghana where the water that comes out of the tap never gets below pleasantly warm. Sitting in those icy baths and swimming in the icy waters off Brighton beach in the UK were informative times. The duration of these sessions in these ice water immersions can be anything between five minutes and 40 minutes depending on where your mind goes. The more focused your mind is on something other than the cold the more likely you are to get through it. I once caught myself falling asleep in an ice bath. This is not that uncommon and many ice bathers set alarms to make sure they don't do this. When in these states of focused attention, it is also important to be relaxed. Focused attention and relaxation are the two essential components to meditation. To manage the cold immersions, you are basically putting yourself into a meditative state.

Now let me go back to my Christian mystic phase. During this time I was part of groups of Christians who practised 'Ascension'. From what I can make out, ascension is where your spirit or soul ascends into the mystical realm. Non-Christians might call this astral travel. I won't try and fully categorise the non-physical realms except to say that most experienced meditators would describe lower and higher non-physical states or realms or dimensions or densities. Scientists and mystics alike commonly describe our physical state as the third dimension or density (3D). From what I can make out the nearest non-physical reality to 3D is the fourth dimension (4D). Again, I am no expert in classification but 4D reality seems to have lower and higher realms. The lower 4D realms seem to be where you might find both 'positive' and 'negative' entities, for want of a better description. The realms then continue upwards from 5D onwards. The higher the realm the more 'positive' the experience. The realms also correspond to states of vibration or frequency. The higher the frequency the higher the dimension or density. You will often hear people talk about raising your vibrational frequency and this being a positive thing. There is a correlation between your state of (well)being or consciousness and your vibrational state. In his book *Power versus Force*, David R Hawkins beautifully describes the ascending levels of consciousness.[2] On a logarithmic scale he describes the lower levels from 0 to 175 as being concerned with 'lower' emotions such as shame, guilt, apathy, grief, fear, desire, anger and pride. The higher levels from 200 to 1000 are concerned with emotions such as courage (200), reason (400), love (500), joy (540), peace (600) and enlightenment (700–1000). Many mystics or meditators focus on the positive emotions and raising their consciousness or frequency to the highest possible level.

What is sad is that in Hawkins' opinion most people and societies do not elevate beyond the lower levels of consciousness and most people spend their whole lives at the same level. The dimensional realities seem to correspond loosely to these levels of consciousness, so the higher the dimensional realms, the higher the levels of consciousness. The lower 4D realms encompass negative emotions, as per Hawkins' scale, but as you attain the higher levels of consciousness through breath and meditation so you will have access to the higher dimensional realms. As I mentioned earlier I'm not an expert on realms, dimensions and densities so please forgive me for trying to summarise something that is very complex. Science, however, is not completely ignorant of these levels of consciousness. In 2017 the CIA in the US declassified a stack of information confirming that they had operated units engaged in understanding altered states of consciousness and in particular 'psychic spying'. This clairvoyant activity was directed mainly at the Soviet Union. The CIA programmes of research started by using clairvoyants. They then realised that they could train almost anyone to do what these psychics were doing and coined the term *remote viewing*, to remove any mystical or religious connotation. It would seem that remote viewing occurs on these lower accessible plains of non-physical reality.

During my mystical phase I was intrigued by some of the great leaders in this ascension movement. They were able to pull great insights and knowledge from these non-physical realms with ease. However, what struck me during this period of analysis was how physically unhealthy some of these mystics were. Their physical 3D state of being didn't seem to differ from the rest of humanity. If one can manage such great spiritual feats, why did the body seem to be left behind? Surely the physical body should glow with the light of the celestial engagement? Shouldn't the energy encountered in this etheric realm (the one outside our physical 3D world) carry over into the earthly realm? I guess I was drawing on biblical references to Moses coming down from the mountain and glowing so much that the people asked him to cover his head (Exodus 34). OK, so Moses was up the mountain with God for 40 days and 40 nights and most ascension experiences last anything from minutes to a few hours, but still you'd expect persistent regular ascension-type meditation to yield at least something positive for the body. If it did, I wasn't seeing it regularly in the spiritual leaders in the ascension movement. Some did seem to maintain youthfulness but the majority did not. I started thinking more about the body, first from a biblical perspective. Most Christians see the body as a sort of earth sac that will be discarded when we die and go to heaven. The idea is that the body is our earth suit and is sinful; sin happens in the flesh and when we die we get rid of it. But my questions kept coming: Why did Jesus take his body with him if it was so sinful? Why was the tomb empty on that first significant Easter day? What was so important about his body? And Jesus' body was not the only important body in the Bible. In Jude 9 we see Michael and the devil contending over Moses' body. Why fight over something useless? Then we have Elijah in 2 Kings 2 and Enoch in Genesis 5:24 disappearing and seemingly taking their bodies with them. Couple this with questions asked of us in 1 Corinthians 6:19: 'Do you not know that your body is a temple of the Holy Spirit, who is in you, whom you have received from God?' It sounded to me as though we were missing something when we neglected the body. Of course as a doctor trying to help people live their best lives in their time on earth living in their physical body, the ascension experiences seemed great but also seemed gruesomely lacking for the sick person struggling in their physical body.

It was as this point that I began to focus my meditations on the body. When comparing the modern ascension movement with ancient meditators I found that the difference indeed was the body. The ancient eastern mystics of India, China and Japan did focus on the body.

What I noticed with my emotionally hurt patients was that the body was switched off. Emotional or psychological trauma seemed to shut the body down as a protective mechanism so that they could go about their normal business. In my interview with my friend Barbara she describes what happened when she started to meditate. She had had a bad back and she was advised by a guru type of a person in India to spend 20 minutes a day 'watching her breathing'. Almost immediately after engaging in 'watching her breathing', her body began to open up and for the first time in almost her whole life she could feel her feet on the ground. Many of my emotionally hurt patients live in their heads. I don't mean that they live in a fantasy land, I mean that they experience emotion through the mind and not the body. Many of my patients are very psychically aware. I find this to be true of many patients especially if they experienced trauma as an infant. It is as though the physical body shuts off and the higher mind takes over. This is the part of the mind or consciousness that is in touch with the non-physical dimensions. So, while this part of their consciousness is very awake, the body remains asleep with the trauma locked into the physical aspect of their being.

I found that NMT worked well to wake the subconscious up to the fact that the body was hurting. In addition, if I gave my patients a meditation to practise at home that included the body, the NMT scores would not wane and many times their NMT scores improved during the time between consultations. The patients who improved most quickly were the ones who were able to make meditation part of their regular routine.

I still use NMT. It is an invaluable first step to unlock the process of waking the body up. However, after the first NMT session, I put a major emphasis on body meditation and processing trauma.

But what is trauma? From a definition point of view, I think we can all come up with a pretty good description of trauma as being caused by an injury of some sort. The cause of the injury can be either physical or non-physical. The result of the injury can also be physical or non-physical. For example if I hit you with a stick, that will cause a physical injury. It may also 'wound' you psychologically or emotionally. You may be emotionally hurt that I chose to pick up a stick and hit you with it. You might say that the psychological trauma resides in the mind somewhere so why should the body shut down if the trauma is non-physical? This is because part of memory resides in our physical being. You may or may not have come across stories of heart transplant recipients not only receiving a new heart but also receiving memories from the person who donated the heart. Research scientists have looked at this area and found that our bodies keep a score of what happens to us. The memories may be stored in our cells.[3] The emotional wound from being hit with the stick is likely to register in the mind *and* in the physical body. I expand on this a little later in the book. I mentioned in my book *Diet to Detox* that practically all physical illness has an emotional or psychological root cause. I believe that the frequency of the emotion sets up a resonance pattern in our cells that then attracts toxins to the body. Again, I talk more on resonance later in this book. My theory is that after experiencing trauma the psyche – or my preferred term, Higher Self (the purest non-physical form of you) – shuts down the physical location of the trauma so that it does not interfere with normal daily activities. The body can successfully do this for long periods of time, but I believe that the shut-down part of the body is not completely silent. It gives off a background hum or low-level distress signal and I believe that this correlates with low-grade inflammation in the body. We know that all chronic disease is related to low-grade inflammation in the body. In turn, low-grade inflammation is related to poor gut health (or gut dysbiosis to give it the medical term).

Research shows that early childhood trauma can trigger gut dysbiosis that can be difficult to correct and may affect you later on in life.[4, 5]

So, the reason for writing this book is an attempt to help you to unlock those early 'stuck memories' that set you up for ill health and that seem to be resistant to all physical remedies.

The stuck record that I mentioned earlier is, in my opinion, being emitted from the cellular memory of the trauma. This is the low-level hum that is constantly playing in the background of a person's psyche. It is this record that informs the person's every analytic thought, behaviour and decision. You might have heard talk of the left and right brain and how this informs our behaviour. I believe descriptions of the left and right brain can help us understand what drives our thinking and behaviour. In the early to mid 1900s severe epilepsy was sometimes treated by removal of part of the brain. One such 'treatment' involved removing the part of the brain that allows communication between the left side of the brain and the right side of the brain. This middle part of the brain is called the *corpus callosum*. Interestingly, after these operations patients could function normally. Scientists were intrigued and examined the functions of the left and right brain and found that, rather than being a mirror of each other as you might expect, the two brain hemispheres exist as two completely separate entities. The left brain is focused on verbal and analytic tasks and is able to manipulate information given to it so as to be able to reason. The right brain is more concerned with visual imagery, feelings, emotions and symbolism. The left brain, via the corpus callosum, takes information from the right brain. It then uses this information in its reasoning to formulate a belief system that it can present or articulate to the outside world.

Over the years I have been especially interested in the corpus callosum because of my daughter Hannah. Hannah has Down's Syndrome which comes with an extra copy of chromosome 21. People with

Down's Syndrome tend to have an underdeveloped corpus callosum. In my research I found that listening to music, and more importantly learning to play a musical instrument, helped the corpus callosum to grow, which in turn improved the connectivity between the two brain hemispheres. In a beautifully researched article, Duane Shinn describes the benefits of learning to play a musical instrument as a child.[6] The article states that learning to play a musical instrument helps coordination, concentration and memory and also improves eyesight and hearing. For Hannah, learning to play the piano as a child certainly seemed to help coordination, concentration and memory. Music seems to be necessary to fine-tune the whole brain. We need both sides of the brain to function well in our world and yet modern education often emphasises the left brain analytic thinking at the cost of the right brain, creativity, symbolism and 'out of the box' type of thinking.

In the growing child it is the right brain that is activated first. Babies and young children live in a right brain's visual, symbolic world. Words and expressions are taken literally and there is little manipulation of information. Babies and young children have a huge capacity to learn facts, images and symbols which are all right brain tasks. I used this method to help my daughter Hannah to learn to read and to learn facts about her world. This was great as the method of learning does not involve a need to manipulate information which is the left brain task. As the brain development continues, the left brain comes online and is able to take the information that has been learned by the right brain and manipulate it. Children are then able to use right brain information to be able to reason and make sense of their world.

It is my belief that our deepest thoughts and behaviours are programmed into the right brain – the part of the brain that comes online first. I believe that it is this part of the brain that also stores the stuck memories or abnormal trauma circuits. However, as we place the most emphasis on left brain analytical thinking we are not taught how to access the right brain. It is the left brain that gives us our inner running commentary. Unfortunately, this running commentary can become twisted if it is based on information taken from the faulty data gathered in the right brain. I believe this is why simply repeating positive affirmations doesn't always work. If an affirmation such as 'I love myself' is said purely from a left brain analytic position, nothing changes in the person's behaviour if the faulty information – e.g. 'You are unlovable' – is stuck and never accessed in the right brain.

Meditation helps us to access the right brain and also to synchronise both hemispheres allowing the sharing of information.[7] Brain research shows that when we meditate we activate specific types of brain waves (alpha and theta) which seem to be linked with right brain functioning. If our traumas are stored in this part of the brain, how do we reach them given that we live in left brain dominant societies? The answer is to be in a relaxed enough, focused state so that we can access the right brain's subconscious space. Once we are there we need to rewrite the hard drive. What rewrites the hard drive? Love. Remember love represents a higher frequency than the negative frequencies that are part of the old programming. The higher frequency always wipes the lower frequencies. So starting with love is essential. In this book we work our way to love before allowing the body to 'process' the traumatic emotions.

How to use this book

The first part of each chapter gives you an explanation as to why I have chosen this activity. I then give some practise tips to help you get used to the activity. At the end of each chapter I give you a step-by-step guide through the full meditation for that chapter. You can also work in pairs with a partner for the step-by-step guide, where one person reads the meditation while the other persons does it. You can also find the meditations on my YouTube playlist (details on page 1).

Take your time learning the meditation. There isn't a completely right way to get into the relaxed and focused state. By using the practice tips and full meditations you'll find what works best for you. Take as little or as long as you like to do the meditations. If five minutes once a day is all you can manage, then better that than nothing. If 20 to 30 minutes three times a day is what feels right to you, fabulous! Whatever works best for you; try to be consistent and do something every day.

I hope you enjoy the book and I trust that it will help you to move ever inwards and upwards on your life's journey.

1

Breath

Understanding how to breathe is probably the most important part of this programme. This is because breathing is closely related to relaxation. When we think of relaxation, we think of relaxed muscles as well as calm, slow and shallow breathing. However, if we think of being anxious, nervous or in a panic, we think of tense muscles and constricted breathing. When we relax our breathing, the muscles follow.

I use breathing as part of clinical Pilates. For those who have never come across Pilates, it is a form of exercise developed by physical therapist Joseph Pilates to assist injured dancers return to health. It focuses on breathing and the correct use of the core muscles while doing prescribed exercises either on the floor or using special machines. To illustrate how powerful breath work is, I was once helping a lady with low back pain in my clinic. As per usual, I would first look at the way she was breathing. After just a few minutes correcting her breathing, she burst into tears. Just correcting her breathing enabled her to release emotions she had been holding on to and, in turn, this release of emotions facilitated the healing of her back problem.

Sometimes after experiencing shock or trauma, a particular part of the body may go into spasm. The spasm may be obvious if the trauma is large such as being involved in an accident. For example, I have treated many people who have been involved in car accidents. If the car is hit unexpectedly from behind, the person may suffer a sudden forward then backward jolt of the neck and head. This is called a whiplash injury. After a sudden trauma such as this, the neck may go into spasm and cause headaches, as well as pain, numbness and pins and needles in the arms. The person may need to wear a neck brace for a few days and then the physical therapist will work with the person to regain correct movement in the neck and shoulders. This often relieves the situation. However, in a small percentage of people, the spasm may not go away. The person's neck may remain locked with very little movement happening and the pain and altered sensation in the arms may persist. As a junior doctor I used to work at The Royal National Orthopaedic Hospital, in Stanmore, just north of London, UK, on the unit which was designed to help people with chronic pain. This was a special unit because unlike other pain units we were not there to give medicines or injections. We were not even there to investigate the patient's pain. Patients being referred to our unit would have already been thoroughly investigated and would have seen many specialists and have tried many different treatments already. Our unit existed solely to help the patient come to terms with their pain. In other words, we were there to help people to live with their pain. Occupational therapists helped patients to find different ways of doing their job – if they still had one – or to manage the activities of daily living. Physiotherapists would help patients to make the most of the mobility that they already had. Work placement officers helped patients to think of jobs and occupations that they could do while still coping with their disability. Psychologists would talk to the patient and take a detailed history of the patient's life in an effort to help the patient to perhaps see that circumstances in their life may have altered the way they responded to this traumatic incident.

I remember one particular young lady who was in her late twenties and had recently got married. This should have been an ecstatic time in her life but this happy time was cut short when she was involved in a car accident and sustained a whiplash injury. All investigations and treatment options had been explored to no avail. On deeper questioning from the psychologist, it transpired that the young girl had been sexually abused as a child. Her happy life with her new husband was interrupted by the subconscious cries for help. The horror of the abuse as a child took its chance to manifest itself in adult life after the accident. It was as though her stiff neck and spasmed muscles were frozen as if re-experiencing that early trauma. While I found my time at RNOH fascinating and I still respect the work done there enormously, I never really saw patients' pain improve. I guess this was partly because we were not there to help the pain, rather to help the patient live with the pain. This saddens me when I look back now. Perhaps some techniques designed to release trauma may have helped some of the patients to move a little further on in their health journey.

Many of us don't realise that we are permanently in a state of tension. If I ask you right now to review your shoulders, I bet many of you with one breath are able to relax them quite considerably. Holding your shoulders in tension almost certainly will mean that you are not breathing as well as you could be.

We think of breathing as being something that occurs naturally without us having to think about it. It's true that our respiration is under the control of the involuntary, autonomic nervous system, but this doesn't mean that we breathe as we were meant to.

Breathing forms an important part of many meditative traditions. A quick search on the online bookstores will give you scores of books dealing just with breathing. I've read a few of them and tried out many of the techniques. Although I learned how to administer Pilates breathing techniques many years ago, at the time I didn't fully appreciate how to guide my patients through their emotional issues. It was after meeting my friend Barbara in 2018 that I was really inspired to look at breath and healing. I met Barbara when we were both attending a course about mushrooms in Spain. Barbara was intriguing because she would often be found staring at the beautiful scenery for minutes on end.

I plucked up the courage to ask her what she was doing and she told me that she was practising her breath-holding. Barbara is a quietly spoken, beautiful Scottish woman. She is around five feet tall and can easily hold her breath for three minutes. I pushed her to explain why she was doing this and then, once back in the UK, I had her come and teach a series of seminars on breath work to my women's group. She told me how she had not only become healed of a chronic back problem through correct breathing but had also healed some deep emotional issues. You can watch the interview I did with Barbara on my YouTube channel (details on page 1).

Barbara developed her own method of teaching correct breathing. Some of her influences come from the work of Dr Konstantin Buteyko. The Buteyko method teaches us to slow down our breathing and to take shallow breaths and not deep breaths. I especially like the Buteyko method because, although at first glance it may seem counter-intuitive, it makes physiological sense and is easy to incorporate into daily life.

Dr Konstantin Buteyko developed the Buteyko breathing technique after noticing that sick people hyperventilate (over-breathe). He was successful in helping people with asthma by getting them to slow down their breathing. He was also successful in eliminating his own severe high blood pressure condition, known as malignant hypertension. In Russia the technique was known as Voluntary Elimination of Deep Breathing.

In December 2000, according to The Buteyko Breathing Association,[1] Dr Buteyko opened a conference in New Zealand with the following words:

> Before telling you about the basic concept of the method, I would like to emphasise that I describe medicine generally in two directions. One direction is the so-called official western. The other, eastern medicine – in particular is the Tibetan medicine or judd-shi.

It has transpired that the truth is on the side of the eastern medicine which has always stated that diseases occur as a result of diseased breathing. The essence of my technique is however in decreasing the depth of breathing.

You would ask me how. The best way is through relaxation of the muscles that potentiate the breathing action. What then occurs is a sensation of having insufficient air if the breathing is reduced.

These are all the instructions – the whole technique.

In a nutshell Buteyko is saying that disease is caused by tension in the breathing muscles and hyperventilation. So, when we relax the breathing muscles and reduce the depth of breathing, we reverse the dis-ease. This is the 'whole technique'. Quite amazing.

Buteyko's method is counter-intuitive because we think that we should take deep breaths to get more oxygen into our body. But let me ask you this: 'What does a fit and healthy person look like?'

I'm sure you'd agree that a healthy person is one with a healthy complexion, whose breathing is calm and barely perceptible. If you saw someone striding towards you taking deep and heavy breaths, you would instinctively think that there was something amiss with that person. And yet often in exercise or meditation classes we hear the instructor start with the command to 'take deep breaths'. Taking the occasional deep breath is not wrong but persistent heavy breathing is not the natural way to breathe.

The whole subject of breathing and respiration is huge. I'm not going to attempt to deal with the subject in its entirety but I would like to highlight a few points. When we examine what keeps a healthy person healthy, we understand breathing a little better. When it comes to health, most research and medical professions concentrate on the subject of oxygen. Our tissues need oxygen to survive. This is correct. But we also need to look at oxygen's relationship to carbon dioxide. We tend to think of carbon dioxide as a waste gas that should be eliminated at all costs from the body. However, this isn't strictly true and the carbon dioxide level inside the cells actually controls the release of oxygen in our tissues. In the healthy state, to maintain good oxygen levels in the cells, we need a good level of carbon dioxide – too little (which happens after heavy breathing) and the cell holds onto the oxygen which is then not available for the tissues to use. In the healthy state when we take more shallow breaths, the carbon dioxide can build in the cells which can then trigger the oxygen to be released. We can train this process by taking fewer more shallow breaths or via breath holding exercises.

Scientific studies have been done to prove that shallow breathing is helpful and many studies have shown how beneficial the Buteyko breathing method is for asthma in particular.[2] One study examining the Buteyko method reviewed the benefits in people suffering with chronic fatigue syndrome.[3] Some of the benefits included a reduction in anxiety, depression and difficulty sleeping. Of course, if we go back to Buteyko's view that disease is caused by disordered breathing, it makes sense that many conditions will be impacted when we pay attention to the way we breathe.

Ask yourself whether you'd rather walk around taking quick, deep and heavy breaths or slow, shallow relaxed breaths. The people taking the deep heavy breaths at the running track are the ones who are struggling. The people at the front look happy and at ease with their breathing (until the last lap or so).

The Buteyko method suggests taking fewer breaths per minute and the breaths should be calm and shallow with an emphasis on a long exhalation. Stop and count how many breaths you take in one minute. The average person will take 12. A sicker person will take more. As a medical student I was taught that an increased respiration rate is one of the first signs that the body is in trouble. A slower breath rate means that we can extract more oxygen from the breath that we inhale. Interestingly, the number of breaths the average person takes per minute has gone up over the years from 10 per minute to the current 12 per minute. I wonder if this has something to do with our increasingly toxic environments?

Before we delve into some practice breathing, it is important to understand a little about the anatomy of the lungs and the diaphragm. The lungs are like balloons that fill up with air when the diaphragm contracts (tenses). The diaphragm is the main muscle structure that separates the chest from the abdomen. When we take a breath, the diaphragm flattens and increases the available space in our chest. The negative pressure that is created then encourages air into the lungs. So when we breathe in, what's actually happening is our brain is giving instructions to the diaphragm to contract, which opens up the chest cavity and the air enters the lungs automatically.

This is important because we may have got into bad habits with breathing, telling our shoulders to do the movement instead of the diaphragm. When I tell a patient to take a breath, it is very common to see the shoulders rise. But the diaphragm doesn't sit up by the shoulders. The diaphragm is attached to the lower rib cage. Use your fingers to identify the lowest ribs on each side of your lower chest and then follow the ribs as they curve down and around to just above your waist. That's correct: the diaphragm goes all the way down to your waist. In fact, it isn't very far from your hips. At the back the diaphragm sends slips of muscle all the way down to your low back at the level of lumbar vertebra 3 (which is called L3). To give you an indication of where to find L3, put your index fingers on the upper edge of each hip bone, then reach behind you so that your thumbs are touching or pointing to one another. This is the level of L3. Your diaphragm has attachments that go down this far. And yet when we think of breathing, we often think of the upper chest moving. And of course, what we think is then what tends to happen. If the diaphragm is actually situated around the abdomen, when you practise your breathing think of this area expanding and rising gently as you take a breath in. Think of the diaphragm relaxing gently as you exhale. When we breathe we also tend to ignore the back area. The lungs fill both the front and the back of the chest and yet we rarely think of the back moving. Try taking a breath and imagine the lungs as balloons filling up both front and back as you breathe in. Try to keep your shoulders relaxed. The slips of muscle that go down to the lumbar spine are also quite important. Many people when breathing will keep their middle section stiff. This is especially the case for athletes and dancers who are taught to keep this area still and strong to maintain good posture. As a former athlete and dancer, when relearning to breathe I found it very difficult to let go in the middle and low back region. To allow the abdomen to gently rise on inhalation felt all wrong and I still have to remind myself to let go of my lower back.

Do the exercises below to help to establish a good breathing rhythm. Once you've practised the individual elements, you might then try the meditation which should flow smoothly. Try not to count breaths when you're doing the meditation; rather focus on 'following the breath'.

Try this practice

1 **Shifting to the abdomen.** You can practise improving your breathing by sitting quietly for a few minutes each day and simply being aware of how you breathe. At first you may be well aware of lifting your shoulders. However, as time goes on and you learn to relax, you will find the focus of your breathing shifting downwards towards the abdomen. Once you are comfortable, think of the rhythm of your breathing. Let the in-breath be as natural as possible. Let the out-

breath be slow and as long as is comfortable.

2 **Extend your out-breath.** Practise extending your out-breath by pursing your lips and controlling it to make it as slow and long as possible.

3 **The balloon.** Put your hands around your lower chest so that the index points to the front of your chest and the thumb to the back of the chest. As you breathe in and out take note of whether or not there is a mismatch of breathing – either left to right or front to back. Try and adjust your breathing so that there is equal breathing throughout the chest.

4 **Breath-holding.** Practise reducing your number of breaths per minute by performing a breath-hold at the end of the slow and long exhalation. Hold your breath calmly, imagining that even while holding your breath, air is coming into your lungs. When you can't hold it any longer start breathing again but be sure to keep your mouth closed. Once you have recovered your normal breathing pattern, repeat the exercise. You may repeat it around four times over a period of say 20 minutes. Doing the prolonged out-breath followed by the breath-hold will reduce your number of breaths per minute, improve your ability to relax as well as improve your wellbeing. You could also practise this breath-hold exercise when out walking and count the number of steps you can take while breath-holding. After some weeks of practice you will notice a calmer breath cycle, which will greatly assist you during this processing programme. Aiming for three to four breaths per minute is a good goal.

5 **Humming.** When up and about the house you could try humming as part of your breath work. What does humming do? Humming will help you to focus on the task of breathing and imagining and feeling light. If you keep practising the humming, every time you

start humming you will automatically begin to focus on *Breath*. What else does humming do? Humming while performing a slow exhalation and keeping the mouth closed, has been shown to help you to get into a meditative state. This type of breathing is used in *Pranayama* yoga and is called *Bhramari*. If practised for five to ten minutes a day for more than a month, it is said to induce feelings of a refreshed mind and bliss.[4] Not only that, humming has also been shown to be helpful in reducing anxiety and depression, for improving hormonal conditions and improving tolerance to tinnitus. It has even been shown to be helpful in reducing drug dependency. I find that if I feel like I'm coming down with a 'cold' and I do a 45 minute humming session, it seems to get rid of the 'cold' before it has a chance to take hold. Studies have been carried out to determine how humming actually works. Firstly, let me explain that the humming studied as part of the *Bhramari Pranayama* is quite specific. It uses a low tone and is often called *bumblebee breathing*. The mouth is closed and the hum makes an 'm' sound. There is usually a normal inhalation, followed by a long slow exhalation. So, how does it work? A case study found that low-pitched humming increases the level of a molecule in the nose. The molecule is called nitric oxide or NO. Nitric oxide has been shown to be antibacterial, antifungal and antiviral. It was found that humming for one hour before bed and three times during the day was able to greatly reduce chronic rhinosinusitis (running nose and sinusitis) after just four days. In the same case study heart rhythm irregularities were also reduced.[5] One suggestion is that the vibration caused by the humming is conducted through the nose and bones of the head and sets up healing brainwave patterns. It might be akin to a baby falling asleep on the chest of a parent who hums calming lullabies. A Japanese study measured brainwave patterns during humming and found that humming increased gamma wave and theta wave activity.[6] Alpha wave activity also looked to be increased but not as strongly as the other two. Gamma brain wave activity is used to perform higher mental tasks such as problem solving. Theta wave activity is present when in deep meditation or when having waking dreams or when flashing vivid images. Increasing theta wave activity is said to improve intuition, creativity, learning and extrasensory perception. The Alpha wave is associated with a light, relaxed, thoughtful state. So, try humming. Quite apart from the above amazing benefits, I find that humming also helps to keep unwanted left brain chatter away. Try it the next time you're doing the dishes or some other mundane daily task.

6 **Body check.** While out and about check how your body is responding to your current environment. Are you tense? If so where? Breathe and relax. Try humming as you exhale and specifically focus on the area that is tense. Can you feel your feet on the ground? So often we live our lives in our head, playing out scenarios over and over again. Stop and relocate yourself in your body. Start by feeling your feet on the ground. Exhale and relax, being mindful of your whole body and how it feels.

Meditation: Follow the breath

In this practice you are tracking the movement of your muscles as they engage in the breathing action. You will follow the rise and fall of your rib cage and your abdominal muscles as you breathe in and out.

1 **Sit comfortably.** Be upright rather than lying down. When you first start doing this exercise you will find that you will tend to get sleepy or even fall asleep. Try to sit upright if you don't wish this to happen.

2 **Know that you are in a safe space.** You are surrounded by a beautiful light. You are completely loved and completely safe. This image and feeling of being in a beautiful safe space helps you to relax and concentrate on the good/helpful exercise to follow. It also helps your consciousness to anchor itself into a good/positive place that will welcome good/positive thoughts and good/positive energy.

3 **For a few minutes be aware of your breathing.** You may be aware that you are breathing with the shoulders. Allow your shoulders to relax as you breathe. Allow the breathing to settle to the upper abdomen. Be aware of the gentle rising of the abdomen as you breathe in and feel yourself relaxing as you 'let go' and breathe out.

4 **See if you can follow your breathing.** Follow the movement of your lower chest/abdomen as you breathe in. Be aware of the tissues around this area moving and expanding. As you breathe out imagine that you can follow the air as you exhale. Feel the air as it passes through your nostrils.

- Breathe in and 'follow the breath'. Imagine that you can feel and see the air as it seeps through the tissues around the lower chest and abdomen. As you exhale 'follow the breath' as it causes parts of your body to relax. Where does the breath go as you exhale?

5 Relax.

- *Inhale.* Feel and see the breath filling your abdominal space. Exhale. Feel and see the breath causing your head, face and scalp to relax. Repeat this until your whole head is relaxed.

- *Inhale.* Feel and see the breath filling your abdomen and chest.

- Exhale. Feel and see the breath causing your shoulders, arms and fingers to relax.

- *Inhale.* Feel and see the breath filling your abdomen, chest and head. Exhale. Feel and see the breath causing your chest to relax. Repeat this until the whole of your torso both front and back and internal organs feel relaxed.

- *Inhale.* Feel and see the breath filling your head, chest, abdomen and pelvis. Exhale. Feel and see the breath allowing the legs down to the toes to relax.

- *Rest in this space.* As you breathe in imagine that the breath has reached (activated) all of your body. As you exhale feel completely relaxed. Imagine that your fingers and toes are so relaxed that they are tingling.

2

Light

Practice makes perfect with this part of the meditation. Initially when I ask my patients to breathe in light, they often say that they cannot see light, just black. This is normal. When we close our eyes we often tend to 'look' at what we see behind the eyelids. This is often black or, if we are sitting in a well-lit room, we might see lighter shades of black. It's not incorrect to focus on this space. As you begin to relax and follow the breath, you will begin to experience different types of light. In my own personal experience of meditation, when I started, like most other people, all I saw was black. Then after a little while I saw swirls of deep colours such as purple, blue or red. There seem to be different types of inner sight. The most obvious to grasp is what I have just described. The physical eyes, using their seeing apparatus, pick up the colours that are visible when the eyes are closed. However, the more relaxed we are, the more the inner landscape changes. We somehow switch from using the physical eyes to using a different type of mechanism to 'see'.

Research into meditation and light shows that, even though the eyes are closed, the visual part of the brain is active. Research shows that the electrical activity in the brain also changes.[1] The electrical activity of the brain is measured using an electroencephalogram (EEG). As mentioned in the previous chapter, the types of electrical activity are categorised into different wave types as follows: gamma waves, beta waves, alpha waves, theta waves and delta waves.

Gamma waves occur when we are performing a highly focused task that requires problem solving.

Beta waves occur during our normal daily activities.

Alpha waves occur when we are in a relaxed state and when we have our eyes closed.

Theta waves occur in the deeply relaxed or semi-hypnotic state such as when we are falling into a deep sleep or waking from deep sleep.

Delta waves happen when we are deeply asleep.

Researchers found that the seeing of lights occurred when the brain waves were in the alpha and theta states. So you could say that seeing lights during meditation comes about as the result of being in a relaxed state, but there is another part to this theory. In the introduction I mentioned that meditation is relaxation plus focused attention. The research backs this up. When researchers analysed how meditation works they found that most forms of meditation rely on the participant being able to focus their attention on to something. Many people tend to think that meditation is about emptying the mind but this is not quite the case. Research findings show that in meditation you seek to cut out all distracting stimuli, at the same time you also focus your attention on one thing. So, rather than emptying your mind, you are actually focusing your mind. What is the 'thing' that we should focus our attention on? Remember my friend Barbara and the guru who told her to 'watch her breathing'? He was telling her to focus her attention on her breathing. Most meditation practices have this element. They might also have an element of focusing on something external such as a cloudless sky or the horizon or a candle or simply a dot on the wall.

The brain activity will show increased and coordinated activity relating to the focused attention, while suppression of activity (akin to sensory deprivation) in the other brain regions.

In my personal experience of meditation, I see swirls of deep colour and sometimes flashes of light. I will also sometimes see geometric shapes with linear outlines. On other occasions, and less commonly, I might have the impression of seeing a full-on image of a scene playing out in front of me. In meditation research all of the forms I have outlined have been described as visual hallucinations that depict a degree of relaxation and focused attention. It seems that the art of meditation is a skill, which can be learned just like other skills, and the changes are visible on the EEG readings.

In Zen Buddhism, a slightly different description of light is given which is called *inner light*. The experience is associated with a sense of being 'blessed' by this inner energy. The brain patterns for this type of light do seem a little different from the average types of light I have described. As well as the alpha and theta waves being activated, there are also bursts of high frequency beta rhythms. Researchers believe that this type of inner light experience represents an even deeper level of relaxation and focused attention.[2] Zen Buddhists believe that this inner light is a reflection of their true self and is the source of health and bliss.

In more practical terms, my belief is that when we first start on the meditation journey we try to relax but we're not that good at it. Our eyes see what is behind our eyelids – black or shades of black, depending on the ambient light. As we become more relaxed, or if it is very dark, we begin to see the swirling deep colours. As we learn to relax further our brain wave pattern changes to the alpha wave state and then the theta wave state. It is here that we may see dots and flashes of light and shapes with linear outlines. I believe that these states are fluid and as our concentration levels fluctuate we may happen upon deeper levels of meditation where we get the 'movie screen'. Perhaps as we become more practised at relaxed attention we may even experience episodes of inner light.

Law of attraction and light

So, in this part of the meditation, what I am doing is akin to the *Law of Attraction*. The Law of Attraction states that our thoughts or ideas are energetic and the things that we think are attracted to us – rather like the Bible verse, 'As a man thinketh in his heart, so is he' (Proverbs 23:7).

If you practise meditation for long enough you will begin to see lights. However, in order to accelerate this process, I am asking you to focus your attention on 'seeing' light, so that light will be attracted to you. By telling yourself to breathe in light you are setting this up as a thought or idea. The quantum field does the rest.

This is how it works. As we are relaxing and following the breath, at first we see the black and then the swirls or we see the black and swirls all at once. We then shift our attention and tell our body to breathe light. When I say 'breathe light', you might think that I mean to breathe light from the outside of yourself through your nose and into your body. This is not incorrect but what I'd like you to imagine is that there is a light situated inside of you. Imagine a small ball of bright light sitting in the depth of your being or deep in your abdomen (just below the stomach). As you breathe in, the light gets bigger. When you breathe out, instead of imagining the light going out into the air, imagine it being sent into your body – through the organs, the bones and soft tissues and out through the layers of your skin. At first you may not 'see' this light and again, this is perfectly normal. However, as you get practised at relaxing and focusing on what you are doing, your imagination and your seeing will merge into the same thing. As you imagine the ball of light getting bigger in your abdomen, imagine what it *feels* like as you follow the breathing in and out. The ball of light gets bigger and you *feel* the warmth and mild tingling as it continues to grow and fill your abdomen. Take your time when first practising this as it's not always easy to follow the breath and imagine the light all at the same time. And of course, you're not in a rush – 'the race is not to the swift' (Ecclesiastes 9:11). Eventually, as you become more practised, this act of focusing on the breath and then the addition of focusing on the light, brings your attention into sharp focus. Importantly, it also keeps stray, left brain thoughts at bay. Following the nuances of the breath seeping into different parts of your body and then picking up the sensations of the light as it fills your being will occupy your right brain. A running commentary from the left brain is difficult to sustain while you focus on breath and light. However, in the beginning it may not be easy to keep out the 'clever left brain commentators'.

What techniques can you use to deal with the unwanted left brain discourse?

It is common at the beginning of a meditation session to have many thoughts rushing through your mind. You can at first simply let them come, knowing full well that you will not think too deeply about them or act on them. You might watch them float into your inner space and watch them as they float out again. It's easiest to do this with trivial thoughts that deal with everyday needs such as the need to pick something up from the grocery store or the need to cancel an appointment.

You may not be able to visualise your thoughts. Most thoughts will happen as if you are having a conversation with yourself. You may 'think' that you're doing very well focusing on the breath and the light and then without warning you will notice that you are having a conversation about it with yourself. When this happens – it will happen often – merely restart the focus on the breath and light. The more you practise this the easier it gets. You may also find it helpful to get into the habit of thinking a pre-arranged thought as you are settling down to do your meditation session. When my children were little, they never wanted to go to bed. Life was just too interesting. Then when they got in bed, they would fidget for long periods of time. I got into the habit of preparing them to be able to fall asleep. I would say things like, 'Shall we get ready for *lovely, comfy, sleepy* bed?' I was suggesting to their minds that going to bed was a beautiful experience where they would fall easily into a peaceful sleep. You can do the same before your meditation session. Tell yourself 'Ahh! I'm going to a beautiful, happy space', or something that resonates with you. Prepare yourself to have a beautiful experience.

Bliss Bubble

If the thoughts are more of a substantial or criticising nature, you might need to be more prescribed about what you do. I often advise my patients to use the *Bliss Bubble* technique for these. For example, the voices may be saying things like, 'This is a useless task. I don't know why you bother', or 'Better not get your hopes up, things will never change.' For this type of harsh commentary, you might still try, and indeed be successful, watching or listening as the comments come in, all the time remaining detached from them, as if the dialogue doesn't belong to you. However, to ensure that you deal with this criticism in a more specific way, you could put the whole commentary into a Bliss Bubble. The Bliss Bubble is beautiful and brightly coloured. You'll need to imagine this. Imagine a brightly coloured, sparkly bubble (or however you wish to 'see' it – some people see the Bliss Bubble as a clear, see-through bubble). See the negative script going into the Bliss Bubble – safe and nicely encapsulated. Then watch as the Bliss Bubble drifts further and further away from you. As it drifts away, it's getting smaller and smaller until eventually you can't see it any more. You are then free to refocus on the breath and the light.

Clearing your energetic (or morphic) fields

It's common to think that our memory of events is stored in the brain. I was taught that at medical school. However, some scientists suggest that memory is not stored in the body at all. Rupert Sheldrake is a world-renowned biologist who I heard speak at The Water Conference in Germany in 2019.[3] Rupert Sheldrake presents compelling arguments for the theory that memory does not reside in the brain. He uses an analogy of a TV set. A child may watch TV and believe that the projected images represent little people who live inside the TV set. Scientists may remove a crucial part of the TV set and when the images fail to appear, they then proclaim that the mechanism producing the images lies within the TV set. Of course we know that the source of the image comes from outside of the TV. He says the same is true of memory. Our brain is simply a tuning device like a TV. Of course if we have an injury to the brain, this is rather like the broken TV part. The brain injury will cause faulty tuning of the messages that come from outside of the body. What is this 'outside' arena? I guess the old fashioned term for it would be the *ether*. This term for the energy and frequency in the space around us fell from use when science started to believe that the world was made up of matter or – in lay terms – solid things. The idea that energy, vibration, frequency in the air that surrounds us could direct what happens to solid matter was seen as absurd.

Sheldrake uses growth and development as an example and argues that our reliance on DNA to do everything can't explain how the body grows and maintains itself. He points out that all cells in a body have the same DNA. How do the limbs know how to become arms and legs in one part of the body and the heart know how to grow into a beating pump in another part of the body? If the DNA tells the cell proteins what to do and all cells have the same DNA, there must be another 'something' that directs the different body parts to grow. He suggests that it is the energetic fields around the cells that inform it of what to do or how to grow. Sheldrake calls these fields morphogenic or morphic fields.

He argues the same thing about memory. Memory, he says, does not reside in the brain but in the morphic field. Many meditation traditions also believe this but may call the energetic field something else. I also believe this. Sheldrake says that we tend to call upon or resonate with our past memories. How do our past memories reside in the morphic field? Well, many scientists who research into the ether suggest that time behaves differently in the ether and that past and present memories (and future probabilities) reside in the morphic field. When Sheldrake says that we can resonate with memories in the morphic field, this may be similar to the Law of Attraction. If we did something in the past and we are thinking of doing a similar thing in the future, the current thought form will resonate (or connect) with the thought form or action from the past. It is my belief that our own memories and any memory that pertains to us resides in this ether.

Water and memory

Let me introduce another concept about memory. At The Water Conference I learned that water also holds memory. What seems to happen is that our DNA gives off a frequency or resonance (I like to think of it as a song) which is then encoded into the body's cellular water. It seems that our cellular water has an enormous memory capacity. How does this fit with Sheldrake's morphic field? Let me try and bring the two together. Let's think about our email on our phone or computer. No one would suggest that the email on your computer is not real. It is there at a click of a mouse. However, a bit like Sheldrake's TV analogy, the email itself is actually stored somewhere else either in the 'Cloud' or on a server somewhere at another location. I believe the memory stored in the body's water (inside our cells) is a reflection of the memory that is stored in our own personal 'cloud' in the ether.

This is all very interesting but what does it have to do with light and meditation? What I notice with my patients is that the pattern of thoughts that they have are governed by their own experiences of life and often from childhood. Also these thoughts may have influences, or echoes, that seem to come from their father or mother or even further back in the genealogy. Scientists working in the field of the subconscious recognise that the space around us is not filled with 'nothing'. Many scientists debate about whether or not our minds, and therefore our thoughts, are actually situated in our head/brain or are actually located outside of the body – just as I explained earlier about memory. Many, including Rupert Sheldrake, would say that our thoughts reside in the morphic field or ether around us. Our thoughts are shaped by our past experiences, but they might also be influenced by other similarly resonating (thought) clouds in the ether. As our DNA sits in our cellular water, it gives off the frequency that links up to the thought cloud. Of course we share DNA heritage with our family, not just those living but those long since passed. This means that we are likely to have a collective cloud that represents the thoughts of our family both past and present.

This even applies to our pets. It would seem that we can share a thought cloud with our furry friends. In one of Rupert Sheldrake's books he talks about why dogs know when their owner is coming home. You and your pet have shared resonance or a shared frequency thought cloud. Your pet will pick up your thoughts in real time. This is a real phenomenon that even happens with plants. Cleve Backster was a scientist who worked on the development of the lie detector test. In his book *Primary Perception* he describes an experiment where he hooked up his yucca plant to frequency detection equipment, simply to see what would happen.[4] He noted that the equipment began to pick up a frequency (resonance) that signalled his planned actions before he actually moved. The weirdest thing about the seeming communication with the plant was that if he moved the plant to the next room it still seemed to pick up his thoughts. This was true even if he moved the plant to another city, even to another country. Rupert Sheldrake would argue that once you have a resonance or connection with a thing, this energetic link (or thought cloud as I would describe it) remains in the morphic field. When it seems as though my patients' behaviours and decisions are controlled by unseen forces, it is my view that there is a resonant connection being made by energetic forms (thought clouds) that reside in the field around them.

I probably haven't done a very good job at describing the real quantum physics behind this but I'm hoping you can catch my drift. What I'm trying to do by breathing light in and through the cells of the body and out into the surrounding ether is to clear, at least temporarily, this sea of unseen 'voices'. By being in a relaxed state and focusing on breathing light, we are creating a resonance with light and excluding resonance from the current of past memories. Rupert Sheldrake says that when we create something new, we are, in effect, creating a new energetic thought form in the ether. After creating this energetic form in the field the first time, this memory remains there for us and others to draw upon for subsequent events. He says this explains why when someone first invents something new, another inventor, even on the other side of the world, will do the same thing very soon afterwards. The thought clouds do not occupy a physical location; rather, they exist outside time and space. He says the same is true in sport. Some years ago I had the great pleasure of meeting Sir Roger Bannister. Sir Roger was an alumnus of the medical school I attended. He is famous because he broke the seemingly unbreakable four-minute mile record in athletics; within a month, the record was broken again. Sheldrake would say that once the precedent was set, anyone else thinking about doing the same thing could draw on the morphic memory to assist them.

My theory is that by flooding our morphic field with new light, we create a new light memory. This is devoid of any old voices. My theory is that as we are relaxed and focused on the light, this new light memory will be particularly strong. When we are intentionally focused, our thoughts *and* feelings/emotions are involved. We can focus on something but it doesn't necessarily require that our emotions are also involved. I believe that as emotions involve 'feeling' and 'feeling' involves our body, when we are intentionally focused we are more able to activate our physical body. Our physical body is what carries our cellular water. It is the water that resonates or sends out a frequency pattern. As we continue to practise sending out the same frequency pattern into the ether, we are creating stronger and stronger links with this field. You can imagine your mind as being a bit like a garden. You have the old plants that have been there for a long time. Perhaps these plants were there when you arrived at the house. These plants were perhaps planted by someone else. You would now like to grow some new plants. You first clear some space and then plant a new shoot. You then continue to water and nurture this new shoot until it is fully grown. Then when you walk into your garden you are drawn to this beautiful new plant. I like to think that this is one of the things that we're doing when we breathe light. We are creating our own new space in our etheric (non-physical) field. This is also why it's a good idea at the beginning of the meditation session to immediately start thinking of your beautiful, happy, space.

Five-minute or more practice sessions

1 You are in your beautiful space – completely loved and completely safe.

2 Practise sitting and watching what happens behind your eyelids.

3 Practise imagining different colours, shades and brightness of colours.

4 Practise breathing light and seeing yourself as a ball of light. What does it *feel* like? You could try and describe the sensations. Some examples of descriptions might be tingling, fuzzy, warm, energetic. See if you can find other words.

5 Practise seeing and feeling light in different parts of your body. What does it feel like? Can you move the light and feeling to another part of your body? Yes, with practice you can.

Meditation: Breathe in light

1 **Sit comfortably.** Be upright rather than lying down.

2 **Know that you are in a safe beautiful space.** You are surrounded by a beautiful light. You are completely loved and completely safe.

3 **For a few minutes watch your breathing and relax.** Allow the breath to fill your whole body. As you breathe out 'let go' and feel your body relax as you concentrate on each part of your body from your head down to your toes.

4 **Breathe light.** As you breathe in imagine a small ball of bright light sitting in the depth of your being or deep in your abdomen (just below the stomach). As you breathe in, the light gets bigger.

  - When you breathe out, imagine the light being sent through the body organs, through the bones and soft tissues and out through the layers of your skin.

  - As you see the ball of light getting bigger it spreads through your body, completely filling it. What does the light *feel* like?

  - Feel the warmth and mild tingling as the light continues to grow and fill your body.

  - Feel the sparkling and energy as the light seeps through your skin and to the surrounding area.

  - See the light as it forms a ball of beautiful light around you. What bright colours do you see?

5 **Rest in this space** as you continue to breathe and 'let go' – remember to check back at certain areas of your body to check that they are relaxed, e.g. the head, shoulders and abdomen.

6 **Be!**

3

Love

When working with my patients, I often speak about the need to engage with 'love and light'. In the past, during guided meditation, I would ask the patient to breathe in 'love'. As we will see later, 'being in(side) love' is the foundation step required in order to 'process' trauma. As we sit inside the energetic force of that which represents love, we are 'in love'. From this 'place' we can then begin to integrate or 'process' the trauma that we have experienced and that exists as an energetic imprint or 'memory' in our physical body.

Most people don't have a problem imagining light. Light and colour are all around us. But what is love? This, of course, is a huge question which I'll touch on only briefly. In the English language we only have one word for love but as we know, love comes in different shapes and sizes. I think that we can agree that a mother's love for her child is different from the romantic love between two adults. The love between siblings or very close friends is different from the love – if indeed you would call it that – we might have for a new possession like a new car or a handbag.

So initially, when I started out in my work helping patients to 'process' trauma, I thought it an easy thing for them to enter into the feeling of love. However, I soon realised that patients have differing interpretations for 'love'. Some may not be able to define what love is to them and others have no real concept of love at all. It is easy to assume that everyone can relate to what are generally accepted as 'definitions' of love. For example, many think that to be loved is to be 'unconditionally accepted' as for a couple in a marriage, where 'love' coming from their spouse is seen as being an unconditional acceptance of their personality – good and bad, with no strings attached. This unconditional love is not unlike the love a mother has for her child. I believe it to be a perfectly reasonable way to define one type of 'love'. However, I can run into trouble with a patient if this type of unconditional love springs to mind when I, as the therapist, mention it during guided meditation. Let me explain. If the patient I'm dealing with has been through a traumatic childhood, this ideal of unconditional love may never have been experienced. It may just be a longing. The patient may long for unconditional acceptance from the parent who was never able to give it. This scenario is very common. It's as if we were programmed to receive unconditional love and if we don't receive it, we are left with a deficiency of that love or longing for it. This then means that when I, as the therapist, ask the patient to access love (to breathe in love), the person is stuck because they are trying to do something that, thus far, has proved impossible to attain / experience. For example, let's take the person who longs for unconditional acceptance from an abusive father. This patient's ideal for the 'love' feeling may be to receive unconditional acceptance from their father. However, they have never actually received this love; it is an unrequited longing. If I then ask the patient to breathe in love, they will be unable to do it. They may simply go 'black' in their inner vision or 'numb' or worse still, the feelings of unrequited love from their abusive father may surface. The feelings here may include anxiety or anger.

After I discovered this potential stumbling block, I realised that I needed to find a gentler, more consistent way to access 'love' without provoking the very trauma I was trying to help the patient deal with. I needed to find a simpler introduction or starting point for 'love'. So, instead of 'love', I now start with 'a good thing'. I know, that seems vague, so let me explain a little further. I believe that all good things emanate from love. I believe that love is the universal good. So if we start by looking at something that we, ourselves, know to be good, it is my belief that it will lead us to the ultimate good which is love. In my practice, this does seem to be the case. The person who suffered trauma as a child and cannot imagine the feeling of unconditional love *can* access something 'good', like seeing a beautiful landscape or the feeling of walking along a sun-kissed beach or taking the first bite into ripe fresh fruit or hearing a beautiful piece of music. To me, these are all aspects of the universal love – given to us as gifts so that we are able to experience the wonders of this life. If we contemplate and 'feel' these introductory gifts for long enough or deeply enough, we are able to gain access to the deeper truths of the universal love.

So, if I ask you to tell me what (non-sexual thing) feels good, what would you say? To me, it's food – something like Devon ice cream. The ice cream made in Devon in the South West of England has an amazing creamy texture that lingers long on the tongue and leaves you feeling good about life.

Describing the physical sensation of a 'good thing', like a taste of your favourite food, is a great place to start but even this may be diffi-cult at first. We tend to be good at describing 'bad' things like pain. As a doctor, I was taught to interrogate people about their pain. For exam-ple if someone has a pain in their lower back, I would ask, 'Is the pain burning, stabbing, throbbing or like electric shocks?' I would then ask if it is a constant or intermittent pain and where in the body it travels to. We have all experienced pain and most of us have had to describe the nature of that pain to someone else. So, although we may be very adept at describing pain, we don't normally describe the physical prop-erties of a 'good thing'. We might say that the ice cream is delicious or tasty but these words do not describe the *physical* effect that 'delicious' or 'tasty' has on the body of the ice cream taster. Similarly you might describe eating your favourite food as 'comforting' or 'soothing'. These words are really describing an emotion rather than a physical sensation. What does 'comforting' actually feel like? What does 'soothing' actually feel like? This can be difficult to put into words. However, it does come with practice.

The physical location of a feeling is also often overlooked. We tend to assume that when we feel a feeling, that feeling is felt all over our body or somehow in our head. But actually, once we begin to get better at describing the physical nature of the feeling, we will see that often the feeling is felt in specific areas of the body and the physical nature of the feeling is quite distinct. Why is this so important? Well, when we begin to 'process' our trauma, we do this from a base of love. I believe that trauma can be held as an energetic imprint in different parts of the body. I will explain more about this in the next chapter but it is important to know that **trauma dissolves into love** when we learn to process it correctly. However, for this to work, we need to be able to **physically** feel love. I don't think that I have had one patient who has not had difficulty describing the physical sensation of love. Not only that, most patients, as do most of humanity, find it difficult to grasp and, therefore, feel love. Why is that? I don't know. Maybe humanity has suffered some type of collective trauma that has caused our bodies to physically shut down. The memory of trauma stored in our physical body is rather like a folder being filed in a certain cabinet in our office. The folder, or memory, is stored in a specific location. You might have heard of people talking about bitterness being stored in the liver, heartache in the heart and shock in the stomach. I don't look for patterns like this when trying to help my patients as my role is to help them to identify the physical location themselves. Let me go back to the folder analogy. The body will try to keep this folder under lock and key so that the information contained within it does not disturb its daily functioning. For example, we may experience a shocking event as a child and as the event is so shocking/traumatic the psyche will try to protect the child from the full impact of this trauma by storing that memory in the body somewhere – let's say it is the stomach. However, while stored in the stomach, the psyche will cause the body to almost ignore that particular area; it will be as if that part of the body does not exist. The memory is under lock and key. In this way, the child can continue its playful and joyful life without being sent off course by this awful memory. The body can indeed do this very successfully, but the trauma folder *is* still there in the stomach cabinet.

Let me give another analogy of how the energetic imprint of the trauma is stored in the body. Our bodies are mostly made up of water. The water is highly organised in our cells and in our tissues, forming a matrix or grid of memory. Imagine this matrix to be like a city grid all over your body. The trauma may reside in one of the houses in this grid. The psyche may learn to ignore this house but the house is still there. In the house may be living some pretty destructive individuals – people having raucous parties, drinking and taking harmful substances. The psyche, or the city police, ignores all of this for the sake of the whole body, because unlocking the road to the house will result in mayhem in the whole city. In the same way for the child, the psyche ignores the trauma sitting in the stomach so that the body does not have to cope with the resulting shock and potential shut down.

What I see with my patients is that people who have suffered childhood trauma are often stoical individuals who sometimes seem to be oblivious to pain. They often make great soldiers and athletes because they can push their bodies to extremes and not feel pain. Their physical bodies are numb – under lock and key – walled off. I believe that this happens to all of us to a greater or lesser degree. All sickness has a traumatic root. The psyche covers up the trauma so that we can live normal lives, but the damage from the deranged energetics does a silent harm to the body. We are 'numb' in this location and so do not feel the disorder until the body begins to feel pain. Pain is the end result of a long journey starting from trauma through dis-order to dis-ease and pain.

If you've ever heard accounts of people who have suffered great trauma as children, you will sometimes hear them speak of out-of-body experiences. They may say that during the traumatic event, their soul/spirit would leave their physical body and rise up into the ether – sometimes being comforted by a great light or divine figure. Their physical body undergoes the trauma but 'they' themselves do not feel the pain as they watch the scene from above. The soul/spirit then returns to the body once the trauma ceases. These descriptions are dramatic but I believe that trauma sufferers to a large extent live 'outside' of their bodies. They may not experience a true out-of-body state but the physical body is so shut down as not to be noticed. In these situations, feelings are not felt physically, they are felt somehow emotionally in the 'head'. Patients who are highly educated are often able to describe these emotions well – as if all of the analytic description is happening above the shoulders, but everything from the neck down is numb. If we wish to be free of our trauma and pain, we must first unlock the memory folders in the body. This involves being physically present in our bodies and being able to feel the physical sensations that go on in our bodies.

Why did I ask the question 'What non-sexual thing feels good?' Let me explain. Often, and particularly for men, if trauma locks down their physical body the only release, or ability to feel physical exhilaration, will be sexual. It can be very difficult in this situation to distinguish the physical sensations that go with love from the physical sensations that go with lust. In fact, there is no difference, the body doesn't distinguish – a tingly sensation is a tingly sensation, the feeling of butterflies is butterflies. To the man it feels good and 'good' to him is 'love' so this experience must be love. Of course, there *is* a difference but if you have never experienced the deeper, fulfilling, all-pervading feeling of love then you have no comparison to make and therefore the superficial version becomes love. I don't want to give men a hard time here. I believe that the physical body is made for love and it will try to stimulate itself into an exhilarated state even when the body is shut down. The psyche uses extremes to do this such as pornography, overeating, shopping, alcoholism, gambling etc. I'm not an expert on addictions but I do notice that these activities do seem to be substitutes that stimulate the physical body, albeit briefly, in a search for that 'love' feeling.

That was quite a detour away from Devon ice cream. But it was necessary because love is the key that unlocks the locked cabinet. Love is the key that opens up the no-go area and cleans up the unruly neighbourhood. But how does ice cream fit in? Well, if food is the only non-sexual way you get to experience 'good', then we start with this as you will see that food can be a gateway to deeper love experiences. This is not permission for gluttony and if food is a severe addiction for you then it may be best to start with something like a situational scenario such as sitting in a beautiful place or listening to your favourite piece of music. This exercise is an invitation to savour and enjoy your favourite thing! Let's get back to the practical aspects of 'feeling' as I delve deeper into the physical sensation of tasting Devon ice cream. See if you can imagine the taste as you follow my description.

I take a scoop of the creamy, already melting, ice cream from the tub and savour the smooth sensation on my tongue. If I wait a few seconds I can feel the creaminess travelling first to the back of the tongue and then spreading out as it passes through the throat. At the same time, there is a gentle explosion of sensation that flows upwards first to the centre of my skull before spreading like a fine, gentle fizz all over my head. This stream spreads downwards both inside and outside my body, embracing almost every part of me, leaving a smooth, fuzzy, tingly feeling as it passes down the front and back of my body and eventually reaching my fingers and toes. This sensation almost feels as though it is an electromagnetic buzz that comes through my skin giving me a momentary external glow.

Were you able to follow my description? How did it feel for you? Forgive me for this indulgence, but my description reminds me of the quote from the cartoon film *Ratatouille*. The young chef Linguini addresses the famous fierce food critic Anton Ego, who has come to his restaurant. Linguini says: 'And you're thin for someone who likes food.' Ego responds: 'I don't "like" food; I *love* it. If I don't love it, I don't *swallow.*'

Maybe you have a food that you really love. Now it's your turn to try and describe what 'good' feels like. *Imagine* that you are taking a mouthful of that food. Let the food rest on your tongue, what do you *physically* feel? Where does that 'taste' go after it leaves the tongue? It is likely to spread to different places. How would you describe the *physical* sensation of that 'taste'? Have a go. It can be useful to do this with a friend or partner. Push them to come up with words – no matter how non-dictionary they sound – that describe the physical sensation and location of the taste.

The easiest way to start is to identify the location of 'good'. Where in your body do you feel the 'good'? It's easy to start with food because at least you know that you're putting it in the location of your mouth. So when you ask yourself the question 'Where do you feel the good?' you can confidently say, 'The mouth'. Again, with a tasty food, you can also relatively easily feel where this good feeling is going. The simplest place is down your throat and to your stomach. You can (mostly) feel this as it happens. However, if you 'sit' in your stillness, you may also 'feel' the sensation moving to different places. I mentioned ice cream goes to my head after the mouth. See if you can identify where your 'good taste' goes after the food hits your mouth. The next step we can take is to try and describe the physical sensation of 'good' as it pertains to the food. Like pain, we perhaps can identify some words that describe the physical sensation of 'good'. However, unlike pain, we're not really accustomed to describing the physical bodily properties of 'good'.

Let's try and create a fresh vocabulary for what 'good' feels like. If you're stuck, an easy place to start is with the feeling of excitement when something 'good' is about to happen. What does that 'feel' like to you? Think back to your childhood when you were jumping with eager anticipation of an event like a birthday or a trip. See if you can get 'in touch' with one of those memories and re-feel the physical sensations. If you struggle to recall a good childhood memory, think of a scenario of excitement from adulthood such as the joy at getting a new job or indeed a new piece of clothing. For me, as a child, waiting for Christmas is one such good memory. My arms and legs would feel fizzy and jumpy, and I would feel flutters and fizzing or popping in the stomach. The words I've used such as 'flutters', 'fizzy', 'jumpy' and 'popping' are not your regular words that you'd find in a dictionary to describe 'love'. Here I've described the anticipation of an exciting event. If I were now to describe what 'good' *tastes* like when eating food, the sensations may not be as intense as if waiting for an exciting event, but they may be similar and more subtle.

Let's go back to food. Once you are able to describe the physical sensation of the food and the location of this physical sensation, you might also want to add descriptions such as the shape, colour and even sound that that sensation evokes. Have a go at this. The more you practise the better you'll get at it. Once you are able to sit in this sensation, all you need do is stay with it, keep feeling the feeling. If you do this with the food exercise, you'll find that once you've felt and traced the sensation, if you sit with it, you'll find yourself in a place of peace and calm or some other description of the emotion of 'good'. It's as if the food unlocks a deeper place inside of you. I believe this is the love journey. We know that food is a comforter – just think of a baby soothed to sleep after feeding. We have descriptions of food such as *soul food* or *love food*. Who doesn't love to go out to a restaurant for a good meal? Food makes us feel good. However, what I'm asking you to do is to take this gift to the next level. I'm not asking you to take five minutes of meditation after every mouthful. No; the beauty of this exercise is that you don't even need the physical food, you can just imagine the food and the body will respond in almost the same way. In fact it's better not to have the food. That way you don't have the torture of looking at the plate of food getting cold as you savour each mouthful. Practise your love journey and see where it takes you.

After food, you can practise with an image or a scenario or listening to your favourite piece of music as I mentioned above. For example, you might choose to be in a beautiful valley, surrounded by spectacular mountains with the sun casting a magical shadow across the lush green valley floor. Your emotions might be those of calm, peace, exhilaration, joy etc. Let's now include the physical body in that experience. Feel your feet on the ground in that place. Try to describe where in your physical body you are experiencing the good sensation of being in that place. Use some made-up vocabulary to describe the physical sensation. Is the sensation just one sensation or more than one? Is it a static sensation or does it move? Does the sensation shift around the body? Does it have a colour, a specific shape or a sound? Enjoy the scenario as you explore it with your physical body. Sit in it, rest in it. At first, of course, it will be difficult to feel the sensations, but with practice it will come. Soon, as you practise feeling, you will find an expanded experience of life. When you are sitting in a traffic queue or find yourself bored, try practising the good feeling. What you're doing is practising creating an energetic field of 'good' around yourself. This 'good' journey takes you to love. So, as you learn how to breathe in the 'good', the journey will take you to a deeper level, to love. You can then breathe in love.

Meditation: Breathe in love

1 **Sit comfortably.** Be upright rather than lying down.

2 **Know that you are in a safe beautiful space.** You are surrounded by a beautiful light. You are completely loved and completely safe.

3 **For a few minutes watch your breathing and relax.** Allow the breath to fill your whole body. As you breathe out 'let go' and feel your body relax as you concentrate on each part of your body from your head down to your toes.

4 **Breathe light.** As you breathe in imagine a small ball of bright light sitting in the depth of your being or deep in your abdomen (just below the stomach). As you breathe in, the light gets bigger. When you breathe out, imagine the light being sent through the body organs, through the bones and soft tissues and out through the layers of your skin. What does the light feel like as it spreads throughout your body? See and feel the light as it forms a ball of beautiful light around you. What bright colours do you see?

5 **Rest in this space** as you continue to breathe and 'let go' – remember to check back at certain areas of your body to check that they are still relaxed e.g. the head, face, shoulders and abdomen.

6 **Breathe love.** As you breathe in you *feel* love sitting in the depth of your being. As you breathe in and out, sit and continue to feel as love swirls and moves in the centre of your being. Allow love to fill your whole being. Enjoy this space of love. Allow yourself to love you. What do you see? What do you feel? What do you hear? Do you taste anything?

7 **Rest in this space** and enjoy!

4

Recognising trauma

How do we recognise we have trauma that needs to be processed? One way of knowing is to ask yourself if you are completely at ease, relaxed and comfortable with yourself and your life and the world and people around you. I suspect that you wouldn't have got this far in the book if your answer to that question was 'Yes'.

Check your body right now or while you're doing a daily task such as doing the dishes. Stop mid-action and check to see if you are relaxed or tense. Which parts of your body are tense? Can you feel your feet on the floor? Do you have a knot in your stomach or your throat? How is your breathing? Are you breathing with your shoulders up? Is your breathing relaxed and slow or tense and fast? Are you breathing with your mouth open or closed? Is your face relaxed or is part of it tense? Are you clenching your teeth? When sitting, is your bottom relaxed or tense? Checking your body like this will inform you of some of the tensions and traumas that you are silently holding.

Of course all emotional pathways pass through the left brain and therefore can be rationalised. The type of person who tells you they have no fear, anxiety, panic, random anger or sadness has either done an enormous amount of inner work or has emotions that are completely shut down. The person who tells you that they are completely happy with themselves and has only good thoughts for the rest of humanity may truly exist, but the majority of such people exist in a type of denial with the true feelings kept under lock and key in the body. Most of humanity harbours trauma which can lead to periods where we might experience random fears and anxieties. We may become accustomed to distracting ourselves away from these fears but they are there nonetheless. All negative energy symptoms such as fear, anger, sadness, anxiety and panic – to name just a few – have a traumatic root cause. The root is often found in childhood or in the womb or even before the womb. Studies show that trauma survivors can 'pass on' the effects of trauma to their offspring. Dr Vivian Rakoff was the first to show this in the children of concentration camp survivors in a research paper written in 1966. Here is a quote from that study:

> The parents are not broken conspicuously, yet their children, all of whom were born after the Holocaust, display severe psychiatric symptomatology. It would almost be easier to believe that they, rather than their parents, had suffered the corrupting, searing hell.[1]

On one level, to process trauma is to face our fears. The traumas are locked into the body and the psyche does its best to keep them there. The psyche successfully ignores this negative energy. Each time that the body attempts to uncover this trauma, the psyche tries to shove it back under wraps. Sometimes this response is associated with feelings of panic. It is rather like being strapped to railway lines, unable to move as a train approaches. As you hear the distant rumble of the train, first anxiety rises as you realise that the rumble represents danger. Anxiety gives way to panic as there is a full realisation of what is about to happen. Circumstances in your life may give an indication that a hidden trauma is about to be exposed. The low-level anxiety may be the signal you need to change the subject or manufacture a distraction. If these do not work the anxiety may increase and a further, more dramatic distraction is necessary. If the anxiety or distraction does not work and it looks as though the 'train' is almost upon you, full-blown panic sets in with attendant sweating, inability to speak or move and palpitations.

A panic attack is just one example of a manifested trauma. The rumble of the train may equally provoke anger or depression. All are signs of a hidden trauma. Panic, anxiety, sadness, tearfulness, depression, frustration and anger may arise for seemingly trivial reasons. Your left brain may try to analyse these random occurrences. It may try to give a logical explanation for the emotional response.

One common refrain I hear from my patients is, 'It's just that…' When the sentence starts with this phrase, it usually means that the left brain is about to construct a reason for the emotional response. It goes something like this. The patient feels hurt, sad, frustrated, anxious or angry about something that someone else is doing or about a situation in their environment or even globally. The left brain excuse is delivered. 'It's just that she needs to realise that she can't behave like that.' This usually means that if this other person stopped what they were doing, the patient could get on with their life and everything would be fine. Of course, that is clearly not the case. What is really happening is that the hidden trauma has 'demanded' an excuse from the left brain. The excuse is there to cover up the emotions that signal the hidden trauma. If you find yourself including this phrase, there may be some trauma that the left brain is trying to cover up for you.

What types of distractions do we use to avoid feeling the trauma?

Distracting behaviours such as overeating, drinking too much, smoking and drug taking are obvious distractions; others may be more subtle. I mentioned earlier that before I understood about the deeper traumas driving ill health, I would be confronted with angry or tearful patients who simply could not give up their favourite foods. A meticulous desire to control the food that goes into your mouth on the severe end of the spectrum may be a signal for an eating disorder such as anorexia or bulimia. However, on a less severe scale it may still present as a distraction from dealing with deeper emotional issues. Sometimes this is immediately obvious but, at other times, it may only be discovered as I begin to work with the patient and there is a tussle or bargaining over which foods can be eaten and which need to be left aside. These interactions sometimes go on to reveal that 'inner child'. There can be a sort of transference that happens. In psychological terms, *transference* describes the situation where feelings regarding old situations or interactions are projected onto the therapist. So, the patient may project on to me the feelings about their abusive mother or father. When I ask them to restrict a certain food, it might trigger emotions related to a person in their childhood. The patient then behaves like the child of their youth responding to the abusive person in their past. This is very real. Sometimes I'm able to point it out to the patient, at other times I will use guided meditation and processing of the feelings to help move past this point.

Other non-food distraction behaviours can be things like obsessive behaviours such as cleaning and tidying up or the reverse such as untidiness or hoarding. Most of us are aware that obsessive-compulsive behaviours are part of a troubled psyche. Most people tend to think of obsessive cleaning or checking the gas as the only features of obsessive-compulsive behaviours. What I've seen in my practice is that the anxiety provoking obsessive thoughts can be of almost any nature. I would class intrusive sexual thoughts that cause anxiety or other negative emotions as one of these distractions. Pornography addiction would fall into this category.

More subtle non-food distractions can be watching TV or social media, reading, listening to music etc. These may seem like normal activities and of course, they are. But if I couple these activities with an avoidance of Self then I call it a distraction. What do I mean by an *avoidance of Self*? Let me explain this a little further. If I ask my patient to close their eyes and 'look' inside, some find this task unbearably difficult. It can provoke anxiety after just a few seconds. Try it and see what happens. The person who finds it difficult to be with Self then finds distractions to make sure that they never have to look inside. They might make sure that music is playing in the background all the time. They may need to play music or read a book in order to fall asleep. They might always have a book or even two on the go. Or in the same way, they might use podcasts and always be listening to something to fill the void, lest it become too scary. They might whistle or sing all the time. Or as soon as they get a spare moment they might be in the garden or flip on the TV or call a friend. They might make sure that their days are filled with activities such as meeting friends or relatives or exercising or shopping. I'm sure you get the idea. How many of us can sit with ourselves and look inside? Perhaps you could take a moment to list your distractions.

Replacement behaviours for lacking emotions

What I have effectively described above are signs that you might have some hidden trauma. Of course we all have. I have also talked about some of the emotions that you might feel such as anxiety, sadness, frustration, anger and panic that might also indicate that there is hidden trauma. I also want to talk about what I call *replacement behaviour*. What is replacement behaviour? It describes the 'good' emotions that are displayed by someone who has hidden trauma. Let me explain why I placed *good* in quotation marks. As I've already explained, when we suffer trauma, particularly at an early age, part of our body 'shuts down' or we could say that this part is numb to emotion. It doesn't or cannot feel emotion. I've described how this is likely to be a protective mechanism allowing the rest of the body to be able to function and get on with normal daily tasks. However, what I see in my patients is that both sets of emotions can be unavailable, both good and bad. I've already spoken about love and how trying to feel love can be difficult if you have not experienced it. I believe that love is the root of all good emotions. This would mean then that emotions such as compassion, joy and empathy would also be lacking.

Let me explain further using an example that is not uncommon in the UK. Boarding schools are a part of UK history. Many people will tell you that their boarding school years were the best years of their lives and they owe their subsequent lives and careers to the fact that they went to boarding school. Some would say that the boarding school environment provided a welcome respite to their lives at home. That said, children as young as six would be sent to live in what many in those days called 'character-building' conditions. In times past these boarding schools were seemingly deliberately harsh, cold and uninviting environments. Parents felt that these conditions would 'toughen' their children up and prepare them for the rigours of life in the outside world. Children slept in large dormitories with very little adult loving support. Food was often scant and of poor quality. Bullying from fellow boarders, and especially older boarders, was not uncommon. Testimonies of physical and sexual abuse emerge more frequently now. Find someone (usually a man) over 50 years old who went to boarding school in the UK and let them explain the gruesome conditions they endured. Boarding schools delivered a product to upper and upper-middle class society. These students became our politicians, doctors, bank managers and judges. But meet one of these upstanding members of the community now and you will find few flaws in their characters and behaviours. Why is this? How is it that a child can be ripped from a loving and comforting home at a tender age when their emotions are still developing and placed in a cold and lonely 'prison' and come out of it in one piece with impeccable behaviour? These 'good' and upstanding qualities are examples of replacement behaviour. They are a display of good manners rather than actions based on good emotions. An old English, or rather French, word for manners is *etiquette*. Wikipedia tells us that:

> *Etiquette is the set of norms of personal behaviour in polite society, usually occurring in the form of an ethical code of the expected and accepted social behaviours that accord with the conventions and norms observed and practised by a society, a social class or a social group.*

The true and good emotions are wiped from these young children's bank of accessible feelings. They are replaced by a programme of expected and acceptable behaviours – the replacement behaviours.

So, my interpretation of the impeccable manners displayed by the ruling elite is that they were meticulously schooled in etiquette. Having been wrenched from a loving environment the body shuts down and no or little emotion is felt. The harsh conditions at boarding school further cement the body's shutdown. The bodily feelings or emotions are then *replaced* by good manners. Good manners or etiquette are essentially a set of rules or programmed behaviours that the children learn. They learn how to be polite, how to maintain eye contact when speaking, how to open the door for a lady, how to wait at the bottom of the stairs while someone is descending, how to listen, how to respond with 'kindness'. These replacement behaviours are quite convincing. However, they fall down when the unexpected happens and there is no code or programmed behaviour for a particular circumstance. You may think that my description is a bit far-fetched; sadly, not at all. There is a recognised pseudo-psychological term for what I have just described. It is called *Boarding School Syndrome*. A psychoanalyst called Professor Joy Schaverien used this term as the title of her book about the subject.

At medical school 30 years ago, I was one of very few students who had not attended boarding school. The behaviour of medical school students was shocking to me – a 19-year-old from a Derbyshire mining village. Drunken debauchery sadly was not uncommon. And yet these same students are now at the very vanguard of medicine. Schaverien describes an ABCD of boarding school syndrome. The A stands for abandonment, B for bereavement, C for captivity and D for dissociation. The abandoned and grieving child is not allowed to display appropriate emotion and therefore pushes it down. In the captivity – i.e. prison – of the school environment they do their uttermost to stay out of trouble and to keep within the rules. Adults with boarding school syndrome display this 'must stay out of trouble' behaviour and are upstanding members of society always seen to be doing the right thing. Dissociation means that the individual develops a split personality (for the non-medical person, a split personality is not the same as schizophrenia). The vulnerable child is left at home and is replaced by the super-confident, almost arrogant, extremely hard-working overachiever. Medical schools were, and still are, full of the latter dissociated individuals. When your physical body is numb you can push yourself to extremes, stay up studying or partying all night and still make lectures the next day. The body is numb and so we need hyperactivity either with sport, drugs, alcohol or sex to give appropriate stimulation. The vulnerable 'child' may stay locked away or come out at seemingly random times at the rumble of the train approaching. This might then be stifled by a suitable distraction such as substance misuse. The university environment often becomes an extension of boarding school followed by the workplace. The programmed 'impeccable adult' is on show for the outside world. The wild 'dormitory child' who parties, bullies and engages in debauched behaviour is often reserved for the trusted group setting. The 'vulnerable child' may stay tightly locked away or at the rumble of the train on the tracks, as I mentioned previously, seek out a suitable distraction.

I know I'm painting a grim picture of medical school but this is what I witnessed. Doctors and vets have some of the highest rates of alcohol and drug misuse of all professionals and the highest rates of suicide compared to the general population.[2,3] Why is this? Alcohol and drugs, both recreational and pharmaceutical, are easily accessible tools of distraction. However, at some point the tension between the various personas becomes just too much for the whole to handle and without appropriate help some find the easiest way out.

The split in personas is a recognised medical term called dissociative identity disorder (DID), which was previously called multiple personality disorder. DID comes about because of trauma in childhood. Each personality is distinct from the others. These descriptions of boarding school syndrome and DID may seem dramatic – after all, not everyone went to boarding school and then off to medical school! Indeed your and my traumas may not be so clear-cut as these but any childhood trauma can provoke similar, albeit sometimes milder, symptoms. You may have had the privilege of having both parents at home during your childhood. However, if one parent was always working and the other parent was at home but not really interested in your thoughts or feelings, the wound you suffer may be one of neglect which may result in feelings like the A for abandonment described in Schaverien's ABCD. Your parents may have provided for all of your material needs. You may have been from a well-off family, living in a beautiful home with as many toys and distractions as you could want, but if there was a lack of love and affection this could result in feelings of not being worthy of affection and a longing, similar to grieving, for love that is not given. The child then does everything that they can in order to attract this attention. This may range from being the 'perfect child', 'staying out of trouble' to getting perfect grades at school or it may alternatively lead to rebellion including substance misuse. There may be similar 'splits' in the personality with one personality being in evidence at home and another when out with friends. On the surface you might say that this is normal behaviour, and it is. However, when the split is accompanied by negative emotions such as abandonment, sadness, frustration and anger then the behaviour may have destructive consequences. Let me give you an example. Two teenage girls tell their parents that they are going to a friend's house while at the same time deceptively packing their nightclub clothes in their bags. They have a great time clubbing and meeting friends. While at the club the girl with the abandonment issues may seek out a boyfriend who seems to fill the hole in her emotions. This boyfriend may then introduce her to substances that magically make all her sad feelings go away. After a few months or years these episodes may take such a grip that they interfere with her life so that she needs therapy. You could say that both girls are playing two roles, their at-home role and their clubbing role. But one girl soon grows out of the idea of being up all night and feeling awful the next day, while the other one actively needs the extra personality which enables her to feel loved, even if it is the wrong type of love.

Of course, as I mentioned at the beginning of the chapter, the trauma may have happened before the child was born. The science of epigenetics describes how genes can be switched on and off. So, for example for diabetes, if the person carries a diabetes gene and it is switched on, the person has a much higher chance of developing diabetes compared with when the gene is switched off. The genetic code itself doesn't change but the on/off switch will determine if the gene is functioning (on) or silent (off).

The research is now clear that there can be an epigenetic change in DNA function after we experience trauma. This epigenetic switch stays in 'trauma on' position and can get passed down through the generations. If this is the case then it makes sense that whole populations may suffer the consequences of some past trauma. Think of wars, famines, slavery and similar hardships. If these shocking experiences were perpetrated on whole populations then surely this, like the concentration camp experience, could be passed on to future generations. Think back through your generation's or country's history. I'm sure you would struggle not to find some degree of famine, war or strife. Surely we are all served with some degree of epigenetic trauma, let alone that which we experience once we are born. How do we right this wrong? Can we reverse this inherited trauma? How do we flip this epigenetic switch back and how do we clear our present day body from the effects of these abuses? I believe that love is the key. It is from this base of love that we then can look at the wounds and erase the scars.

I've described many different types of trauma and how they originate and how they manifest. My descriptions are not exhaustive. I've mainly described the types of trauma I have come across in my professional practice. So, how do we finally deal with trauma? In the next chapter I will talk you through the final and practical steps in this love journey.

5

Processing trauma

Dealing with trauma is actually quite straightforward once you have become adept at sitting *in love* or sitting *in 'a good thing'*. The more you practise being *in love* the more the background energetic field around you changes. When you come at trauma from a background of love, trauma is more easily able to dissolve into love. It may sound simplistic but all it takes to process the trauma is that you face it. Of course this is simplistic but also dramatic. To face the trauma is to bring on some of those 'approaching train' feelings. The key, remember, is to practise being *in love*. You don't need to be perfect at it, but you do need to be able to trigger yourself into some part of love or 'a good thing'. When you then allow yourself to feel or experience the trauma, you will find that in the first instance the feelings will not be as dramatic as you previously might have felt them as you are starting in a place of love and comfort, as if wrapped in a warm supportive glow. It's from this place that you allow yourself to experience the feelings of this trauma. This may seem a little scary at first, but after just a few seconds you will see how the experience becomes a positive one very quickly.

Let's try it. Choose a situation or scenario that often leads you into a negative place. It might, for example, be an individual who triggers a negative reaction in you. Perhaps being in this person's company causes those feelings of anxiety, frustration, anger or panic to arise. First of all, go through your preliminary steps of breathing, being in a safe space, relaxing, breathing light and being in love/a good thing. With practice, it need only take a few minutes or a few breaths to get into this state. Once you are comfortably *in love*, invite your body to experience the physical sensation of the negative emotion or emotions that get triggered in the company of that person or when you find yourself in the negative scenario. Allow yourself to physically experience the emotion. When we give our body the permission to physically feel the emotion or emotions on the background of love, we are supplying the key that unlocks the trauma folder. The love releases the constraints so that you are no longer tied to the tracks and it is then you are free to see the train for what it really is. As you watch it approaching, you will notice that it gets smaller and smaller, until by the time it reaches you it is a small plastic toy train that you can pick up and examine without fear.

Identifying the physical characteristics of the trauma

Let's go back to the physical processing. In the same way that we learned how to feel 'good', we now learn how to identify the trauma. You may start by *locating the position* of the trauma in the body. It can be anywhere, although the most common areas seem to be the stomach, the chest and the throat. *The physical feeling* may again be almost any sensation but the most common seems to be a tightness or constriction and sometimes a numb feeling as though there is simply nothing there – a black hole. Knowing that you are sitting in love, allow yourself to physically experience the trauma; relax, breathe and let go into the physical feeling, knowing that you are completely loved, safe and secure. Doing this is likely to provoke sadness and tears. Let this happen. Allow the tears to flow as you relax, breathe and let go in love. You may also find that although the sadness comes and you feel on the point of tears, the tears won't flow. Don't worry about this. In time you will learn how to 'let go' and allow the tears to flow. Keep monitoring the physical location and the nature of the pain of the trauma. It may start out in one location and have a particular characteristic, for example it may start out as a black constricting tightness felt in the chest. Then, as you let go, you may notice that the *colour changes* and the sensation may have some *movement* to it. For example it may start to swirl or become like a moving thread. As the colour and movement change the tightness may lessen. Stay with it, breathe, relax and let go, knowing that you are in a safe place, completely loved and in love. You may find it helpful to switch between breathing light and love and then going back to feeling the emotion of the situation. As you continue switching between love and the trauma, you will notice that the trauma emotion lessens.

During this process, as you identify the location and nature of the pain, you may wish to gain some further insight into the nature of the trauma. At this point you may ask for *Higher* Help. I refer to this Higher Helper as my *Higher Self.* You may identify this helper as The Divine, or God or the Holy Spirit. Whoever or however you trust to gain this deeper insight, go ahead and ask for some clarification about the nature of the trauma. You might ask, 'What is this?' Your Higher Self may respond with a momentary single word or flash of encouragement as the pang is being worked through. This moment of intuition is coming from the right brain. Be careful not to allow your left brain to scrutinise what is going in too much detail. The Higher Self speaks through the symbolic and largely non-verbal right side of your brain (unlike the left brain). There will be no long back and forth dialogue or in-depth analysis – just a momentary flash of knowing, an image or flashback to an event perhaps in childhood or simply a single word. Acknowledging this message from the right subconscious brain may sometimes unlock the tears. Let the tears come and allow yourself to feel the emotion of this moment. Processing the trauma from love can seem a little hit and miss at first, particularly as the part of you responsible for coping with the pain of the trauma (or the psyche) will not want to uncover it. The trick is to lock on to the negative emotion as soon as you experience it. Don't allow a 'distraction' to cover it up. Take the preliminary steps to love and then allow yourself to focus on this negative emotion. Again the psyche will want to ignore the pain of this emotion. This is normal. Allow yourself to sit in love then try again with the painful emotion. Where is it located? What colour is it? Does it move around?

The process may take just a few minutes if the trauma is superficial and perhaps occurred just recently. On the other hand a deep-seated childhood or generational trauma may take a while. You might need to sit for some minutes allowing yourself to feel the pain of the emotion and allowing tears or sadness to manifest. For many of the deep-seated traumas, you may not process them in one session. This is normal. The way to manage a deep-seated issue is to call it a day when you feel that you have finished that session. I normally don't suggest that the session lasts for more than about 20 minutes and for most people less than 10 minutes is enough for one session. When you sense that enough time has passed for that session, tell yourself: 'That is enough for now.' As you breathe, imagine that the trauma is a stone that you have in your pocket. At the end of the session take the imagined stone out of your pocket and look at it. How big is the stone? As the sessions progress the stone will get smaller and become more translucent (see-through). Once you have taken a mental note of the size and translucency of the stone put it back in your pocket. You may then re-examine it after the end of the next session. At the end of the processing session bring your attention back to love. Breathe, relax and be in love for a few seconds as you reset your energetic field. You may want to count yourself out of the session. Either silently or out loud, count from 5 to 1 slowly. Before you start counting, tell yourself: 'Every day, in every way, I'm getting better and better and better and better.' Then tell yourself that as you count from 5 to 1, when you reach 1 you will feel physically and emotional great, fully alert and ready to continue on with whatever you were doing. Feel your feet on the ground or your bottom on the chair, then open your eyes; you are now ready to get on with what you were doing in the knowledge that you have done some appreciable work on processing the trauma. Well done!

The Personified Trigger

What is it that triggers the negative reaction in us? We may be seemingly 'triggered' by a person. The presence of that person or conversation with that person may trigger a negative reaction in us. For example, spending time with that individual may be a source of irritation for us or hearing that person's voice may cause anxiety or anger. Even thinking about that person may set you off.

What I'd like to draw your attention to is the location of the trigger. The voice, physical presence or thought seemingly flip a switch in you that then results in the anger, frustration, irritation etc. Where is the switch, the trigger? Is it external to you – somehow residing in that person – or is it internal to you, in *your* being? I would suggest that the switch or trigger is in you. It may be easy to think that if this person could just change their ways then you wouldn't be triggered. If *they* could be nicer or more gentle in their approach to you or somehow see the world the way you see it, then *you* wouldn't be triggered. This way of thinking is common in my patients. The thoughts are usually directed at a parent, sibling, partner, a boss or some significant individual or individuals in the person's life. The patients often have a quest to bring this individual or individuals to task. They want to make the individual see that their actions have resulted in harm. The internal dialogue might go something like this: 'If dad could see that the way he treated me as a youngster has caused me so much pain now as an adult, I would be able to resolve my trauma and move on with my life.' The patient often wants the person they see as the trigger to admit their 'wrong doing', in a sort of 'truth and reconciliation' type of reha-bilitation. However, this journey is often fruitless and results in a circular type of mental torture for the patient as that person does not change (and sometimes is not even aware of what they have done wrong).

I often ask the patient to think of what would happen if the person they view as the 'trigger' of their ill-being were to die. Surely those negative feelings would still be there, forever causing pain and destruc-tion. If that person were to die and the negative cascade of feelings could still be switched on, this suggests that the switch, the trigger, is not in the individual who died but in the individual still alive. If the person who caused the initial trauma is now dead, neither the memo-ry nor the emotions of the trauma disappear. And even though this person is dead, the negative cascade of emotions can still be triggered by something – an event, a movie, an image or another person. The trigger is an internal phenomenon. The trigger is inside of you. Remove the trigger and you remove the cascade of negative emotions. I call the individual who flips the switch the *Personified Trigger*. That person may indeed have been responsible for the initial trauma. On the other hand the Personified Trigger may be someone that reminds the psyche of the initial perpetrator of the trauma, even though they themselves are not the originator of the initial trauma. In this way the Personified Trigger behaves a little like a ring tone on your mobile phone. The Personified Trigger has a very special ring tone that is alerting you or flipping your internal switch to relive the negative cascade of emotions associated with the initial trauma.

So, the Personified Trigger may be the original perpetrator of the trauma or may be someone who triggers the same reactions as the original trauma or someone that reminds the psyche of the original person that initiated the trauma. For example, the original perpetrator of the trauma may have had a certain way of scratching her nose. If you encounter someone who scratches their nose in the same or similar way, it may trigger the cascade of negative emotions. You may be completely unaware that the nose scratching similarity was the trigger, you might just feel that 'That person triggers me'. No matter who the Personified Trigger is, and no matter whether they know or not that they 'trigger' you, the switch is still in you. We can work on the internal trigger so as to switch off the 'ring tone' and at the same time the internal switch. This in turn will deal with the negative cascade of emotions. So, once we recognise that the trigger is inside of us, we can begin to take responsibility for our reactions to certain situations and begin to have control over the outcome. One way of looking at this is that the original trauma situation set up an energetic switch inside of our body. Every time it is flipped, the switch results in a cascade of negative reactions which result in negative emotions. This, in turn, results in disordered functioning in our bodies, which left unchecked results in dis-order, dis-ease and pain.

What constitutes the switch?

I've already mentioned the renowned researcher Luc Montagnier. He won a Nobel Prize for his work discovering HIV. Previously I spoke about his work on the memory of water. Montagnier and others have shown that water in our body behaves like a liquid crystal and is so arranged that it has an enormous capacity for memory. At the Water Conference I attended in 2019, Luc Montagnier said:

'Water is part of our DNA. To transmit information you need water.'

It is my belief that the 'switch' is energetic in nature. It is a configuration of the water in our system. I mentioned in the previous chapter about the studies on Jewish Holocaust survivors. Studies showed that the children of survivors were more likely to suffer post-traumatic stress disorder (PTSD) compared with children of Jewish parents who did not live through the Holocaust.[1] The 'trauma genes' which sit in the water matrix are switched on. I mentioned previously that the switching on of the genes is called *epigenetics*. This epigenetic configuration is then passed down to the next generation.

If it is water that holds the DNA, the 'switch' is likely to be made up of an epigenetic change in the DNA-water matrix. This doesn't answer the question of why different emotions seem to be 'held' and felt in different parts of the body, but I'm sure the answer to this question will be revealed to us in due course. Describing the 'switch' as part of our genetics – which are passed down through the generations – may make it seem that there is nothing we can do to change it. This view would be incorrect. We *can* change our genetics. Or rather we can change the switch. It is our environment that causes the switch to get flipped. For example, you could have a genetic test that revealed that you have the genes that cause diabetes. This could be a source of great sadness. However, you may live your whole life without ever succumbing to diabetes. Why could that be? Because if your diabetes genes are not switched on, you don't get the disease. This very fact is the reason why so many DNA testing companies went out of business. Simply looking at your DNA will not determine your future.

OK, but what if you already have the genes switched on – then what? Well, you can switch them off again. I go into more detail about how and why genes are switched on and off from a biological perspective in my book *Diet to Detox*. Briefly, inflammation, infections and toxins help to switch genes into their destructive state. If you get rid of the toxins, improve your gut health and reduce inflammation, your genes will flip into their positive states of function. And the same is true of the psychological toxic and torturing thoughts that keep us locked into a trauma state; they switch on the destructive gene-water epigenetic state but we can reverse this state too. The gene-water configuration doesn't really distinguish between a destructive thought and destructive chemical. How come? This is because the destructive thought comes first. The destructive thought is an energetic state which is communicated in energetic form – rather like a spark plug in a car. The energy of the thought or emotion is then translated into the biochemical and physiological systems of the body. In this changed state, the configuration of the water may then be such that it now welcomes or attracts the attachment of toxins. Let me try and explain this a little further. Two people with identical bodies drinking the same polluted water may not experience the same reaction. If only one of those individual's body has a configuration that encourages the attachment of toxins, then that person will become unwell while the other may stay well – if such a configuration to attract toxins is absent. The psychological state influences the configuration of the gene-water matrix rather like a 3D jigsaw puzzle. In the normal state the matrix may not be able to hang on to toxins, but once the configuration is changed by negative thought patterns, the new configuration may now easily attach itself to the toxins. The big question is:

If we change our thoughts, can we alter our DNA?

The answer to this question is a resounding 'Yes!' A paper by Glen Rein describes how focused intent can cause changes in the folding of our DNA.[2] The DNA folds in a similar fashion to folding paper into different shapes. The folding of the DNA affects how it functions. It likely affects the signals and energetic field that are then generated around the DNA-water matrix. When we succumb to random fears such as the pang of anxiety when we are about to run out of money as we watch our bank account slip into the red, are we engaging in a self-fulfilling prophecy? Could it be that we are creating the very conformational change in our DNA-water matrix that actually attracts poverty? And what if the reverse is true? Can thoughts of abundance cause a similar DNA-water energetic change to attract abundance into our lives?

Some of you may think this is all a little far-fetched and are sceptical that just thinking certain thoughts can have such power. This is completely understandable. However, studies do show this is possible and I see the transformation in many of my patients. Why not give it a try?

Below is the meditation to assist you in processing trauma. By now you will be familiar with the stages that lead up to this point, the stages that lead up to love/a good thing. Be sure to practise these preliminary stages until you are confident that you are feeling at least some love. For quite a few people, being *in love/in a good thing* all by itself will help to deal with the trauma. Then, coming to the final stage will really be a much more gentle process.

Meditation

1 **You are in a safe beautiful space. Breathe and relax. Breathe light and rest in this space. Breathe love and rest in this space.**

2 **Give permission to yourself to bring up the negative emotion or situation.**

    a **Location.** Where in your body to you feel it?

    b **Colour.** Does it have a colour?

    c **Motion.** Is the feeling static or does it move around?

    d **Feeling.** What does the emotion physically feel like – e.g. a tightness, dull ache, numbness, heaviness etc?

3 **Allow yourself to sit with these feelings.** Focus on the location, colour, motion and feeling as you continue to breathe. The feelings may have a particular characteristic, e.g. like a dagger or sharp object going down the back, or as though you have been punched in the stomach or weighed down by a heavy object.

4 **Ask your Higher Self what the feeling represents: 'What is it?'** You may receive an immediate answer with single words such as betrayal, abandonment, bereavement, shock etc. This insight may unlock deeper emotions and tears. Let them flow. Remember, if you find yourself having an internal dialogue, this is your left brain trying to analyse the situation. If this happens, take a few breaths of relaxation, light and love and restart.

5 **Go back to love.** Breathe love after sitting with the negative feelings for a minute or so. Then switch back to the negative emotions or relive the scenario that provoked the emotions. You will find that the characteristics of the emotion will change. The location, colour, motion and feeling will change.

Sit with these new sensations and again ask the Higher Self what these new feelings represent. If the sensations are part of something already mentioned, you may not receive a further answer. In this case continue to breathe and monitor your body to see what happens to the emotions. Stay in this place for a few minutes. Be patient and kind to yourself and allow whatever emotions you feel to surface so that you can acknowledge and feel them.

6 **The stone.** You may be able to completely resolve the trauma in a short session of a few minutes. On the other hand if the trauma is deep-seated or complex with a lot of layers, you may want to stop after 10 or so minutes. Tell yourself, 'That's enough for now.' Take the imagined stone which is 'the trauma' out of your imagined pocket and look at it. Take a mental note of the size and translucency of the stone. This will give you an idea of how much work there is still left to be done on this trauma. Once you've looked at the stone, put it back into your pocket.

7 **Back to love.** Go back to love and breathe love and light and sit in your beautiful space until you feel energetically relaxed and light.

8 **Count yourself out from 5 to 1.** Before this you might say to yourself, 'Everyday in every way, I'm getting better and better and better and better.'. Then tell yourself that as you count from 5 to 1, when you reach 1 you will feel physically and emotionally great, fully alert and ready to continue on with your day. Feel your feet on the ground or your bottom on the chair, then open your eyes, you are ready to get on with what you were doing in the knowledge that you have done some appreciable work on processing the trauma.

9 **Well done!**

Processing on the go:
The Four Breaths technique

What happens when you are out and about and have no time to sit down and get into a relaxed state? You can do the Four Breaths technique. You may have that momentary pang of anxiety I mentioned earlier, i.e. about money or something else. Someone may inadvertently 'trigger' you, perhaps while out driving or you feel the 'train approaching' during a conversation. The Four Breaths technique will take you very quickly into love so that you can process what just happened and move back into love.

The Four Breaths technique works if you have already been practising through all the stages of the meditation. The body will quickly be able to relax, breathe light and love and be ready to process. Here's how it works.

1 You are in a safe space. Put yourself into your beautiful place as you take the first breath then breathe out.

2 Breathe in light with the second breath and as you breathe out imagine a wave of relaxation and light spreading from the top of your head down to your toes.

3 With the third breath breathe in love and enjoy this feeling as you breathe out.

4 With the fourth breath you are then ready to process the emotion. As you breathe in notice the location, colour, movement and feeling. As you breathe out, let it all go, relax and see yourself in your beautiful place.

6

Moving forward

Trauma is a malady that affects us all. In writing this book my hope is to bring the simple steps to releasing trauma to a wider audience than just my patients.

It may be tempting to focus on Chapter 5 – the processing trauma chapter – but the earlier chapters of this book are just as important, and it is essential that you read these. You will find that by focusing on breath and relaxation, light and love, much of your trauma will simply cease to exist. You might also find that if you set out to deal with some very specific negative emotions or triggers, as you work through breath and relaxation, light and love, these emotions or triggers are dealt with before you even get to work on processing the trauma. By engaging in breath and relaxation, light and love on a regular basis, you are in effect resetting your energetic field. By getting into the habit of following your breath, relaxing every part of you, breathing light and then love, those background negative voices have no anchor to your energetic space. And the more you practise, the better you get at focusing your attention on your Self and the better you get at this, the more able you are to change the DNA-water conformation. Just a small amount of practice, say 10 minutes per day, will set you up in the right direction to reset your Self. Gradually, over time, you will realise that you feel better when you are focusing good intentions on your Self and you will positively seek to do this at any spare given moment. As you begin to focus on just breath and relaxation, light and love, you will begin to feel different sensations in your body. At first you may find that old injuries surface; this is because injuries are trauma scars that have not been completely resolved. As you continue with the inner work, your Higher Self will guide you as to how to correct the injuries or sicknesses. This might be by just more focused intent or it might be that your Higher Self directs you to people who can help you or a combination of both. As you continue to practise you may also begin to notice sensations that you have never felt before. Sensations such as feeling a draft of air when there are no windows open or feeling heat or warmth around different parts of the body or sweating and feeling goosebumps – these are some of the common new sensations you may feel. Focus your intention on these new feelings and see where they take you.

You might also find that you will feel differently around people in your circle of friends and family or when out in public. You may feel that you are no longer in tune with people who you were very close to previously. You may feel that you no longer want to frequent the places that you previously loved to go. On the other hand you may find that you are being introduced to people and places that resonate more with your new Self. Imagine that your energetic Self is a musical note or a song. The song that was your old Self may have been a heavy rock song and your new song may be a completely different genre of music such as reggae, jazz or classical music. If our song changes and we used to resonate with people or locations that played rock music, we may now not feel comfortable in this environment. Another way of looking at it is that 'Hurting people attract hurt people'. Once you are no longer hurting, you will begin to attract people who are resonating with light and love songs instead of pain and hurt songs. This can mean that you pass through a wonderful journey in terms of renewing your Self but a painful and sometimes lonely journey in terms of coming into dis-resonance with some of those in your close circle of family and friends. Embrace this change and continue your positive inner journey toward your new Self.

References

Introduction

1   S Jung, O O Buruk and J Hamari. Altered states of consciousness in human–computer interaction: A review, NordiCHI '22: Nordic Human–Computer Interaction Conference, October 2022. doi. org/10.1145/3546155.3546667

2   David R Hawkins. *Power vs Force: The hidden determinants of human behaviour*, Hay House, 2014

3   M B Liester. Personality changes following heart transplantation: The role of cellular memory, *Medical Hypotheses*, February 2020. 2020;135:109468.

4   D A Drossman. Abuse, trauma, and GI illness: Is there a link? *The American Journal of Gastroenterology*, ACG, January 2011. 2011;106:14-25.

5   G Clarke, S Grenham, P Scully P *et al*. The microbiome-gut-brain axis during early life regulates the hippocampal serotonergic system in a sex-dependent manner. *Molecular Psychiatry*, 12 June 2012. 2013;18:666-673.

6   D Shinn. Music & intelligence: Will listening to music make you

smarter? 2005. Available from: https://ezinearticles.com/?Music-and-Intelligence:-Will-Listening-to-Music-Make-You-Smarter?&id=39927

7   K C Khare, S K Nigam. A study of electroencephalogram in mediators. *Indian Journal of Physiology and Pharmacology*, April 2002. 2000;44:173-178.

1 Breath

1   www.buteykobreathing.org/history

2   S Patil, P Shilna Rani, K U Dhanesh Kumar. Implication of buteyko breathing technique in asthmatic population: A literature review, *Journal of Pharmaceutical Research International*, 2021, Volume 33, Issue 58A

3   M Sakharoff. Buteyko breathing technique and ketogenic diet as potential hormetins in nonpharmacological metabolic approaches to health and longevity. The science of hormesis in health and longevity. In S I S Rattan and M Kyriazis (Eds.), *The Science of Hormesis in Health and Longevity*, Elsevier Academic Press, 2018. doi.org/10.1016/B978-0-12-814253-0.00023-1

4   M Kuppusamy, D Kamaldeen, R Pitani, J Amaldas and P Shanmugam. Effects of Bhramari Pranayama on health – A systematic review, *Journal of Traditional and Complementary Medicine*, January 2018. 2018;8:11-16.

5   G A Eby. Strong humming for one hour daily to terminate
    chronic rhinosinusitis in four days: A case report and hypothesis
    for action by stimulation of endogenous nasal nitric oxide
    production, *Medical Hypotheses*. February 2006.
    DOI: 10.1016/j.mehy.2005.11.035

6   P Rajkishor P *et al*. EEG changes after Bhramari Pranayama.
    Japan Society for Fuzzy Theory and Intelligent Informatics,
    2006. SCIS & ISIS 2006.

2   Light

1   J R Lindahl, C T Kaplan, E M Winget and W B Britton.
    A phenomenology of meditation-induced light experiences:
    Traditional Buddhist and neurobiological perspectives. *Frontiers
    in Psychology,* 3 January 2014. doi.org/10.3389/fpsyg.2013.00973

2   P-C Lo, M-L Huang and K-M Chang. EEG alpha blocking
    correlated with perception of inner light during Zen meditation.
    The American Journal of Chinese Medicine, 2003. 2003;31:629-642.

3   www.globalwaternet.com/news-events/calendar/13639/water-
    conference-2019

4   C Backster. *Primary Perception: Biocommunication with plants,*
    White Rose Press, 2003

4 Recognising trauma

1   R Yehuda and A Lehrner. Intergenerational transmission of trauma effects: Putative role of epigenetic mechanisms. *World Psychiatry*, October 2018. DOI: 10.1002/wps.20568

2   F Dutheil, C Aubert, B Pereira *et al*. Suicide among physicians and health-care workers: A systematic review and meta-analysis. *PloS One*, December 2019. 2019;14:e0226361.

3   S E Tomasi, E D Fechter-Leggett, N T Edwards, A D Reddish, A E Crosby, R J Nett. Suicide among veterinarians in the United States from 1979 through 2015. *Journal of the American Veterinary Medical Association*. January 2019. 2019;254:104-112.

5 Processing trauma

1.   R Yehuda and A Lehrner. Intergenerational transmission of trauma effects: Putative role of epigenetic mechanisms. *World Psychiatry*, October 2018. DOI: 10.1002/wps.20568

2.   G Rein. Effect of conscious intention on human DNA. Proceeds of the International Forum on New Science, Denver, October 1996

Diet to Detox

Diet to Detox explains how crucial a healthy gut is to our wellbeing and how to achieve it.

Symptoms of chronic ill health such as fatigue and aches and pains are due to chronic inflammation. Where does chronic inflammation come from? An unhealthy or 'leaky' gut! So, if we correct the gut, the inflammation goes away. But how do we correct the gut? This is the big question, which leads to another question. Why did the gut get sick in the first place? *Toxins.* Toxins in our environment and in our food help to damage the gut. Dealing with the toxins is the first step on the road to recovery. Adding delicious health-giving fermented foods is the next step. I developed a step-by-step roadmap, to help my patients to embark on the journey back to recovery.

Diet to Detox explains these steps in detail, so that you can take that journey yourself. The recipes at the back of the book will greatly assist you along the way.

Includes 90 recipes

ISBN 978-180042200

Printed in Great Britain
by Amazon

42247824R00059